D0930630

BROADWAY PLAY PUBLISHING, INC.

LOSING TIMES

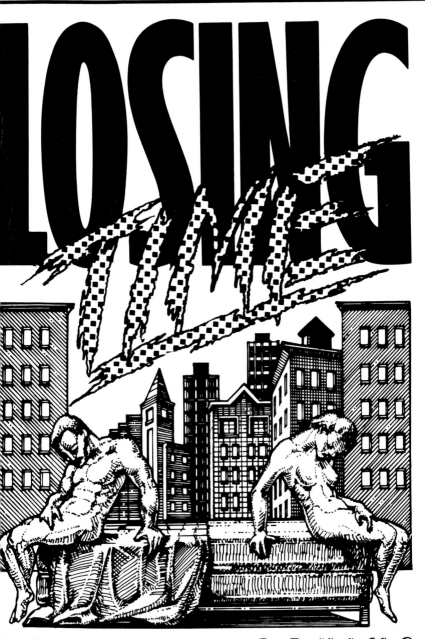

BY JOHN HOPKINS

BROADWAY PLAY PUBLISHING, INC.

Losing Time

by

John Hopkins

249 WEST 29 STREET NEW YORK NY 10001 (212) 563-3820

First printing: March 1983

ISBN: 0-88145-005-7

Cover art by Craig Nealy.
Design by Marie Donovan.
Set in Baskerville by BakerSmith Type, NYC.
Printed and bound by BookCrafters, Inc., Chelsea MI.

For Shirley Knight and Jane Alexander

"It is only by daring the depths of their own souls that women will discover both the inhibitions and the keys to autonomy and truth."
Colette Dowling

Copy of the program of the the first performance of LOSING
TIME as produced at the Manhattan Theatre Club, Downstage
Theatre, on September 11, 1979.

Director .... Edwin Sherin
Set Design .... Karl Eigsti
Costume Design .... Jess Goldstein
Lighting Design .... Frances Aronson
Production Stage Manager .... Amy Pell
Associate Artistic Director .... Stephen Pascal

CAST
(in order of appearance)

JOANNE .... Jane Alexander
RUTH .... Shirley Knight
MIKE .... Tom Mardirosian
WALLY .... Bernie McInerney
TOD .... Tony Roberts

SCENE: Joanne's apartment in New York   TIME: The present

LOSING TIME was first performed in a workshop production
at the Manhatttan Theatre Club. The Artistic Director is
Lynne Meadow. The Managing Director is Barry Grove.

PRODUCTION STAFF

Assistant Stage Manager .... P'nenah Goldstein
Assistant to Director .... Julie Forsmith
Audio Coordinator .... Sandy McIntyre
Assistant to Mr. Eigsti .... Jonathan Arkin
Assistant to Mr. Goldstein .... Nan Penman
Assistant to Ms. Aronson .... Annie Wrightson
Electrician .... Judi Gilbert
Sound Operator .... Toby Simpkins
Scenic Artist .... Kathy Urmson
Production Assistant .... Stephen Helper

ACT ONE

Night.

The living room of JOANNE'*s apartment is on the tenth floor of an apartment building in mid-town Manhattan, on the West Side. The living room has more generous proportions than a modern apartment. The height of the room and the quantity of floor space indicate its pre-war origin. The room is remorselessly square, with sharp and right-angled corners. The other rooms of the apartment open out of the living room.*

The furniture does not reflect any one specific style and the room is not particularly tidy. There are more books than the room can easily absorb. They overflow the shelves and collect on small tables. They gather in the corners of chairs and they accumulate in piles on the floor.

The living room is dark.

Some light spills into the living room, through the bedroom doorway. The sound of a television set can be heard, voices drifting into the living room, from the bedroom, where JOANNE *is lying in bed, reading and casually watching a late-night talk show on television.*

There is a house telephone on the wall, beside the kitchen doorway. The buzzer sounds. It makes a harsh and rasping sound.

There is no response to the sound of the buzzer. The voices continue. It is not possible to hear what is being said, but the intermittent bursts of laughter, followed by applause, demonstrate the nature of the programme.

The buzzer sounds again.

The sound of the television set stops abruptly, as JOANNE *operates a remote control switch. The silence in the bedroom coincides with silence in the living room, as the buzzer stops.*

A police siren screams along one of the broad avenues, which intersect the cross-street and the sound filters through the intervening canyons, muffled, before it travels as far as the apartment, but still a strident intrusion.

JOANNE *steps into the bedroom doorway.*

The buzzers sounds again and the noise drags on, interminably, as JOANNE *hesitates, before she walks across the room to answer its peremptory summons. She takes the receiver off the hook.*

JOANNE: Yes? Hullo? Who is it?

JOANNE *waits impatiently for an answer, glancing quickly around the darkened room, looking for a pack of cigarettes.*

JOANNE: Who's there? For Christ's sake! Who is it? Ruth?

JOANNE *presses the release switch, which opens the front door of the apartment building.*

JOANNE: Come in. Come on up. Have you got the door? Ruth?

JOANNE *waits for a response before she hangs up the receiver.*

JOANNE *switches on a table lamp. She gathers a handful of books and puts them on the coffee table. She begins to tidy the room and then, she abandons any hope of achieving the miracle necessary to make the room tidy before the elevator reaches the tenth floor.*

JOANNE *switches on another table lamp and decides there is enough light in the room, without it seeming to be an attempt to conceal the untidiness.*

There is something frenetic in her reaction to the voice, more to do with her appearance, the impression she will create, something, which reflects a sudden, almost adolescent lack of confidence.

JOANNE *reacts to the sound of the elevator climbing towards the tenth floor. She walks into the bedroom.*

The elevator clatters to a halt, as JOANNE *walks out of the bedroom and hurries across the room, pulling a robe on, over her pajamas.*

The doorbell buzzes, a light sound, in contrast to the harsh insistence of the house telephone.

JOANNE *opens the door and* RUTH *steps, uncertainly, into the apartment.*

RUTH'*s face is dirty and her hair is pulled down around her shoulders. She has been wearing her hair gathered up and secured at the back of her head. What make-up she is wearing has been smeared by tears and there are evident signs of violence. Her coat is torn and one sleeve has several cuts along the forearm.*

RUTH *stumbles as she steps forward and* JOANNE *catches hold of her, with one arm around her waist and the other arm across her chest.*

JOANNE: What happened to you? My God!

RUTH *starts to cry. The tears are less painful to observe than the sobs, which shake her whole body.*

JOANNE *puts her arms around* RUTH, *who rests her head against the other woman's shoulder. The two women are of an almost equal height and general build. They are both in their thirties.*

Instinctively, JOANNE *rocks* RUTH.

RUTH: . . . tried to call you . . .

JOANNE: Christ!

RUTH: . . . didn't answer . . .

JOANNE: I turned the 'phone off!

RUTH: Wouldn't talk to me . . . people . . . told me . . . "Get away!" One man . . . thought I was drunk . . . he said . . . "Fuck off! Go fuck yourself! Bitch!" He spat at me.

JOANNE: I'm sorry.

RUTH: Lost my purse.

JOANNE: Did he . . . did someone . . . take it?

RUTH: No. I had it . . . I remember . . . after . . . and I must have lost it . . . somewhere . . .

JOANNE: After? What after? Where? Do you remember? Do you want to tell me?

The loss of her purse gives a focal point for RUTH'*s more general pain and she begins to weep again.*

JOANNE: Oh, baby!

RUTH: . . . not . . . my fault . . .

JOANNE: It's all right.

RUTH: . . . said . . . the man said . . . if I didn't want . . . I shouldn't walk . . . on my own . . . I shouldn't be out at night . . . walking the streets . . . he said . . .

JOANNE: All right.

RUTH: He tried to cut my face. I put my hands up in front of my face. He was going to mark me, he said. Make it so nobody would ever want to look at me.

JOANNE *senses* RUTH'*s rising panic and tries to control it, physically, holding her, comforting her.*

RUTH: He got hold of me by the throat. He dragged me backwards into this alley. His hands were all over me. Pulling my coat. Pushing up under my skirt.

JOANNE: Didn't you scream? Christ! You should have kicked him in the balls!

RUTH: There were trash cans in the alley. I fell over one of them and the garbage spilled out. He rolled me on my stomach and pushed my face down into all that filth.

JOANNE: God Almighty!

RUTH: I did scream! He pulled me over on my back. Showed me his knife. He put the knife against my throat. He told me, if I tried to scream again, he'd push the knife blade through my neck. He'd cut my head off.

JOANNE: Christ!

RUTH: He took his . . . thing . . . out and I threw up. The smell of garbage, and the stench of him, his body, his disgusting clothes. The vomit filled my mouth. I choked and retched and the stinking mess went everywhere. It covered his hands, his . . . thing . . . it spurted up into his face. He climbed off me. He used my coat to wipe the vomit from his hands. He called me obscene names . . . and went away . . .

JOANNE: What did he look like? Can you remember?

RUTH: I know what he looks like.

JOANNE: You must talk to the police.

RUTH: Talk to them? About him?

JOANNE: If you can tell them what he looks like . . .

RUTH: Oh, no.

JOANNE: You were lucky, Ruth. He let you get away.

RUTH: I won't talk to anyone.

JOANNE: Next time . . . you don't know . . . with someone else . . .

RUTH: It wasn't my fault.

JOANNE: No. Of course! I'm not saying . . .

RUTH: . . . going to put . . . his thing . . . into my mouth . . .

JOANNE: Oh, baby!

RUTH: You can't make me talk to the police.

JOANNE: I don't want to . . . it's not a question . . . no . . . I can't make you . . .

RUTH: I wouldn't have told you.

JOANNE: I just think you have a responsibility . . .

RUTH: . . . had to tell . . . someone . . .

RUTH *takes a step back and away from* JOANNE, *turning towards the door.*

JOANNE: 'Kay! Okay!

RUTH: He had a knife.

JOANNE: Forget I said anything.

RUTH: He was going to cut my face.

JOANNE: We'll talk about it later.

RUTH: Kill me, he said!

JOANNE *touches* RUTH, *gently, and establishes physical contact again, controlling her, calming her.*

JOANNE: Come and sit down.

JOANNE *helps* RUTH *with the buttons on her coat.*

RUTH *reacts to the slight pain of the lining pulling away from the knife cuts on her forearm. The sleeve of her blouse is stained with blood, where the shallow slashes along her forearm bled, first, when she was attacked and again, now, as she tears them open for a second time.*

JOANNE: You're bleeding, Ruthie. Christ!

RUTH *stares blankly at the blood seeping through the fragile material of the blouse. She starts to shake.*

JOANNE *drops the coat on the floor and takes hold of* RUTH's *arm.*

JOANNE: We should have a doctor look at this.

RUTH: No! I'm all right. It looks . . . I guess . . . worse . . .

JOANNE: It doesn't look good.

RUTH: I'm not . . . it isn't . . . I don't need . . .

JOANNE: Will you let me wash these cuts? They can do with some attention. We don't want them to get infected.

RUTH: . . . didn't feel him . . . cutting me . . .

JOANNE: I'll get some water. You stay here.

JOANNE *walks toward the bathroom, hesitates, and looks at* RUTH.

JOANNE: You'll be all right? If I leave you on your own?

RUTH: . . . doesn't hurt . . . not really . . .

JOANNE: Good. I'll be just a moment. *(Laughing)* Don't go anywhere without me.

RUTH: What time is it?

JOANNE: Midnight . . . just . . . a quarter after . . . why?

RUTH: Will you call home for me? Tell Maria where I am. She gets worried. I said, no later than eleven.

JOANNE: You want me to tell her . . . what? You'll spend the night here?

RUTH: No. I can't do that. I must get home. The children . . . in the morning . . . they like me to have breakfast with them, before they go to school. I can't stay the night.

JOANNE: The kids won't miss you. One morning! Christ! It's got to be worse for them, seeing you, looking like this!

RUTH: Will you call? 243 . . .

JOANNE: I've got the number. Yes. I'll call.

JOANNE *walks into the bedroom.*

RUTH *stares at the bloodstained sleeve of her blouse. She touches the blood with the fingers of her other hand and lifts the hand to her face, smelling the tips of her fingers.*

RUTH *raises the arm and smells the blood on the sleeve of her blouse. The sickening odor of the vomit makes her retch.* RUTH *unbuttons the blouse and pulls it off her back, violently. She drops the blouse on the floor and stumbles away.*

RUTH *makes an animal-like moaning sound, as she struggles with the zipper of her skirt, dragging the zipper along its track, unfastening the waistband. She lets the skirt fall on to the floor and steps out of it.*

The moaning sounds become more audible, as the struggle with her clothes becomes more frantic.

JOANNE *steps into the bedroom doorway, carrying the telephone.*

JOANNE: Hey, there! What are you doing? (JOANNE *speaks briskly into the receiver.*) 'Kay, Maria. 'Bye. (JOANNE *hangs up the reciever and puts the telephone on to a small table.*) Here, Ruthie. You'll catch your death.

JOANNE *takes off her robe and helps* RUTH *to put it on.*

RUTH *drags off the rest of her clothes.*

JOANNE: Make you feel better?

JOANNE *leads* RUTH *towards the sofa.*

RUTH: After he left me . . . after I got up . . . I started to run . . . I thought he might come back . . .

JOANNE *settles* RUTH *on the sofa.*

RUTH: I had to get as far from there . . . as far from him! I ran. I didn't look where . . .

JOANNE: You didn't start out . . . coming here?

RUTH: I don't think so. When I couldn't run any more, I

stopped, and I was just along the street. Maybe I was coming here. I don't know.

JOANNE: No one tried to help you? No one asked what happened to you? Christ!

JOANNE *walks into the bedroom.*

RUTH *looks at her hands. She smells the sweet, acrid odor of perspiration on her body.*

JOANNE *walks into the living room.*

JOANNE *is carrying a bowl of water, cotton wool and a towel. She sits next to* RUTH *and puts the bowl of water on the table in front of the sofa.*

RUTH: Some boys ran after me. One of them caught my arm and spun me around. They were laughing.

JOANNE: God Almighty!

JOANNE *attends to the cuts on* RUTH's *arm, gently, and efficiently, cleaning and examining them.*

RUTH: I tried to call you.

JOANNE: I'm sorry.

RUTH: I guess I was coming here. I wanted to tell you.

JOANNE: I'm glad.

RUTH: I didn't think what time it was.

JOANNE: Doesn't matter.

RUTH: I kept pressing the buzzer. You must have wondered . . .

JOANNE: I was in bed. I had the TV on.

RUTH: I thought maybe you weren't here. I started to get sick.

JOANNE: Oh, baby!

RUTH: I couldn't go back out on to the street.

RUTH: That's the last time I switch off the telephone.

RUTH: I guess I would have stayed there. In the hallway. It seemed like the safest place.

JOANNE: These aren't so bad. Once you get the dirt out. You're really lucky. They won't even scar.

JOANNE *touches* RUTH's *face, a simple, instinctive and affectionate gesture, which she can no longer restrain.*

JOANNE: You want to take a shower?

RUTH *shakes her head and* JOANNE *lets her hand fall away from the other woman's face.*

JOANNE: You might want to wash up, if you take a look at yourself in the mirror. I'll find a bandage for your arm.

RUTH *stands up and the robe falls open.* RUTH *seems unaware of the half-naked revelation of her body. She walks into the bathroom and closes the door.*

JOANNE *picks up the telephone and carries it across the room, as far away from the bathroom as the long lead will permit.* JOANNE *sits on the arm of the couch and she dials a number.*

The looping wail of an ambulance siren echoes along one of the avenues. It is accompanied by the harsher, more abrasive sound of a police siren.

JOANNE: Hi! Is Steve there? . . . May I speak to him? . . . Tell him, Joanne. One of his older girl friends . . . . Hi! Did I wake you up? Who's your friend? . . . Christ, Steve, if it wasn't important . . . shit! I don't want to talk to you, any more . . . Right! It's Ruthie. She's in a mess and she needs help. At the very least, she needs someone to take her home. No, Steve. She's not drunk . . . No, she's not asking for you. She's hurt. She's not hysterical. It was my idea . . . . Oh, sure! A bad idea. The best I could come up with at short notice . . . .

Hurt, right. She's been mugged. Damn near raped! Anyway, she's in no state to get herself home and I thought you might welcome this opportunity to work on one of your more undeveloped attributes . . . compassion! . . . Christ! Whatever it is you've got in bed with you, surely, she won't mind? A little care and comfort for your ex-wife? . . . She's not going to be jealous? Over you and Ruthie? *(Laughing)* Doesn't she know? If she's going to be jealous, any woman on the street, between the age of six and sixty. Goodnight, Steve. The leopard doesn't change his spots. Like they say, once a selfish, egocentric prick, always . . . . And you, baby! See you around.

JOANNE *hangs up the receiver.*

She searches through the jumble on the coffee table, looking for a pack of cigarettes.

RUTH *opens the door and walks out of the bathroom.*

JOANNE: Bandages! That's what I was looking for. Hey! Isn't it remarkable what a little soap and water will do for a person? You look much better. How do you feel? Terrible! You're not really going home? I wish you wouldn't. It worries me.

RUTH: Have you got something I can wear? I don't want to put those clothes on again.

JOANNE *walks into the bathroom.*

JOANNE: No problem. Look in the closet. Anything you see. Anything takes your fancy.

RUTH: I'd rather stay here.

JOANNE *walks out of the bathroom.*

JOANNE: Why don't you?

RUTH: What did you tell Maria?

JOANNE: I said that you were here with me and you wouldn't be home for a while.

JOANNE *bandages* RUTH's *arm.*

RUTH: How did she seem? What did she say?

JOANNE: Okay. In Spanish. She was asleep. She wasn't waiting up and worrying about you. She's your maid. She's not your mother.

RUTH: I don't want to talk to the police.

JOANNE: I'm hip.

RUTH: Suppose they catch him . . .

JOANNE: Christ! I hope they do!

RUTH: What's he going to say?

JOANNE: What can he say?

RUTH: He saw me walking on my own. It was late. He thought I was a prostitute. That's what he's going to say. He'll tell the police I led him on. He'll accuse me!

JOANNE: No one's gong to believe him. You can bet the police know the scum-bag. Most likely, he's got a record for . . . this sort of thing. You don't have to be afraid of anything he's got to say.

RUTH: I was on my own.

JOANNE: You didn't lead him on.

RUTH: I didn't see him. The first I knew, he had his hands around my throat.

JOANNE: That's what you tell the police.

RUTH: Have you noticed? Don't I smell . . . like him?

JOANNE: No.

RUTH: I thought . . . taking off my coat . . . my clothes . . .

JOANNE: You don't smell of anything in particular. Certainly not some dirty old tramp!

RUTH: Not old. I don't think . . .

JOANNE: Whatever!

RUTH: Even the robe . . . it seems to have the same . . . muddy smell.

JOANNE: Thanks a lot!

RUTH: At first, I couldn't smell him any more. When I put this robe on, it was fresh, and clean . . .

JOANNE: I should hope so!

RUTH: Now . . . it's like the filth is all inside me . . .

JOANNE: Inside your head! Baby, you have got to get some rest. Stop going over . . .

RUTH: He wasn't old. Not more than twenty.

JOANNE: He should pick on someone his own age.

RUTH: Funny . . . yes . . . I thought . . .

JOANNE: I was joking!

RUTH: He wasn't ugly. Dirty . . . yes, he was. Not someone, like a cripple, someone you couldn't want to touch. His face was angry. Like a child, I thought. His eyes . . . and when he took hold of me . . . (RUTH *brings one hand up to her face and smells her fingers.*) It wasn't having sex with him. Him . . . wanting to put his . . . thing . . . (JOANNE *reaches out and takes hold of* RUTH's *hand. She moves it away from* RUTH's *face.*) I've done that for Steve. Towards the end, the only way . . .

JOANNE: Ruthie, look, I'm really not interested . . . you and Steve. Ancient history, you know. Tell me about this guy. You want to tell me. If it wasn't having sex . . .

RUTH: . . . wanted to hurt me . . .

JOANNE: Sounds like he wanted to kill you.

RUTH: He didn't want . . . sex . . . pushing his thing into my face, holding it . . . like some kind of weapon!

For the first time JOANNE *loses control of her emotions and she lashes out, wildly.*

JOANNE: Why didn't you let him stick his cock in your mouth and bite the goddamn thing in half.

RUTH *retches, violently, and then pitches forward on to her knees, in front of the sofa.*

JOANNE: Oh, baby! *(Puts her arms around* RUTH.*)* I'm sorry. I don't want to make it worse. I want to help. It makes me so fucking angry! I don't see why it has to be you . . . of all people . . . Christ!

RUTH: I was so afraid.

JOANNE: Baby, yes, I know.

RUTH: . . . ashamed . . .

JOANNE: There's no reason . . . you don't have to feel ashamed . . .

RUTH: . . . using me . . .

JOANNE: It's not your fault.

RUTH: The smell . . . his excrement . . . can't you smell . . .

JOANNE: No, I can't. I can't smell anything. You. That's all. Hot, and a bit sweaty. Nothing wrong with that. Not a smell of him.

RUTH: I wanted to tell Steve. When I was running, and I didn't know where, I thought . . . Steve! I'll find Steve and tell him. When he was sitting up on top of me, with the garbage all around, I thought . . . if Steve knows, he'll make this stop. If I shout loud enough . . . if I scream . . . Steve will hear. He'll come and find me. He won't let this man . . . use me. This man can't have me, I thought. I belong to Steve. This man can't put his . . . thing . . . *(Retches violently and coughs, harshly.)*

JOANNE: Christ! Baby, you'll go crazy, if you keep on like this. You've got to stop. Look, why don't we . . . I don't know. God Almighty! What would I do? If it happened to me, what would I want to do? If I'm going to help you . . .

The telephone rings and JOANNE *picks up the receiver.*

JOANNE: Yes? . . . Who is this? . . . What do you want? . . . Yes . . . Is that a good idea? For what it's worth, I don't think you should. *(Offers the receiver to* RUTH.) It's Steve. He wants to speak to you.

RUTH: Why is Steve calling you?

JOANNE: Do you want to speak to him?

RUTH: Does he know? How can he know?

JOANNE: Here! *(Puts the receiver into* RUTH's *hand.)*

RUTH: Steve? . . . I'm all right . . . Did she? When? I didn't know . . . I didn't ask Joanne to call. I didn't want you to know. You think it's just one more of my pathetic attempts to make you come home to us . . . right? . . . Cuts and bruises. Nothing serious . . . Joanne exaggerates. I wasn't mugged. He didn't take anything. I wasn't raped! . . . I don't know exactly. I was walking on the West Side . . . somewhere . . . near the Park . . . Why not on my own? What am I supposed to do? Call up a friend? What friend? The only people I see are the kids. Oh, yes! And the occasional mother. Most of them, like me, left to make out on their own . . . All right! I'm not being fair. I don't feel like being fair to you. Look, don't worry. I'm fine. I can get myself back home. You don't have to come and get me. Is that what you had in mind? . . . God damn you, Steve! Why do you have to sound as if you care what happens to me, live or die, you don't care. You don't give a damn! . . . I don't want to talk to you.

RUTH *lets the receiver slide out of her hand. It falls on to the floor at her feet.*

JOANNE *picks up the receiver.*

JOANNE: You get the message? . . . You really are some kind of an ass-hole! She wants you to come and get her.

RUTH: I don't want him to come and get me. I don't want to see him. I don't . . . ever . . .

RUTH *tries to take the receiver away from* JOANNE.

JOANNE: What do you expect? She's going to beg? Stevie, once in your life, try not to be such a prick! Get your ass over here and take Ruthie home.

RUTH: I won't go home with him. I won't let him take me home!

JOANNE: What? You're going to stay here? Don't be so stupid! Christ! The two of you!

RUTH *wrestles the receiver out of* JOANNE's *hand.*

RUTH: If you can't stop what you're doing long enough . . . if Joanne calls you . . . tells you . . . and you won't get out of bed! *(Hangs up the receiver.)* You don't have the right. God damn it! Why did you tell him? I didn't want him to know.

JOANNE: Go home, will you? Sure! Go home! What am I supposed to say? You think I want you staying here to shout at me? Fuck you! Look, you want your husband back? You want to know something? You'll have to try a whole lot harder. Don't you know that? Being number two, you always have to try harder, right? Climb the Empire State. Jump off the Brooklyn Bridge. Better! Spend his money! Get yourself in debt. I mean, really deep! Tell them you don't have any money of your own, just what your ex-husband gives you. Make him take an ad, disclaiming responsibility for any debts you may incur. Really make him look a shit! Get some smart-ass lawyer in to tell the Judge you've had a nervous breakdown and it's all his fault. Plead temporary insanity! Christ! Let them put you away. What difference? Then he's got the children to take care of, on top of all the rest. You want to make him suffer, baby? Don't get yourself beat up, raped in some alley by a freaked-out kid! He doesn't feel that. You don't hurt him. You only make him angry. Feeling guilty, he won't come back. Break the bank and he just might. It's your best shot.

The telephone rings.

JOANNE: You want to get that?

JOANNE *picks up the receiver.*

JOANNE: What is it, ass-hole? . . . She won't speak to you. You had your chance. You blew it. Why not just go back to sleep? Or did we wake your friend up with all the shouting? . . . I don't know what else to tell you, Stevie. She's right here. She's looking at me, and she doesn't want to talk to you. *(Offers the receiver to* RUTH.*)* He wants to come and get you, he says. He wants to take you home.

RUTH *takes the receiver.*

RUTH: You have to stay with me. You can't take me home and see me into bed, walk out and leave me on my own. You don't have to sleep with me . . . No, you didn't say it. I did. Just so we know what this is all about.

JOANNE: Oh, baby!

RUTH: I'm not looking for a driver. I can call a cab. I want someone to take care of me.

JOANNE: Ruthie!

RUTH: I'm not asking you to come back home and stay with us. Tonight . . . I need you . . . I wouldn't ask . . .

JOANNE: You don't have to beg.

RUTH: Steve, can you wait a minute? *(Covers the mouthpiece of the receiver)* Go away!

JOANNE: You had him.

RUTH: What do you know?

JOANNE: He was on his way to get you.

RUTH: Will you let me talk to Steve?

JOANNE: Don't humiliate yourself!

RUTH: I don't give a shit! You know what I'm saying? As long as he comes back!

JOANNE *walks into the bedroom.*

RUTH: I'm sorry, Steve . . . Steve? . . . I was talking to Joanne. She wants me to stay here . . . What did you say? What are you doing? Why is she laughing? . . . Yes, she's laughing. What did she say? What's going on? Can't you leave her even long enough to talk to me? Can't you get out of bed? . . . What did she say? . . . What is it she finds so funny? Tell her to stop laughing. God damn it, Steve! Are you listening to me? What is she doing? . . . He tried to cut my face open . . . Yes, he had a knife. He cut my arm. He said he was going to cut my throat . . . No, I'm not making all this up . . . No, I haven't talked to the police. I'm not going to. Oh, go to hell! What do you care? For all you care, he might as well have cut me open, emptied my guts out on the sidewalk! . . . He wanted me to fuck him . . . Yes, that's why he dragged me backwards into the alley. Are you listening to me? He sat on top of me. He took his thing out and he wanted me to suck on it. Is that what she's doing? Is that why she's stopped laughing? Has she got her mouth full and can't talk? Oh, Christ! Steve, I want you to take care of me. I'm so frightened. Steve, it isn't possible. I can't make it. I need you . . . really . . . don't you know that! Where were you? Why did you go away? You never told me. I never have understood. Steve? What are you doing? Are you listening? . . . Steve! . . . I'm sorry. I don't mean . . . listen . . . please . . . come and get me . . . take me home . . . look after me. I'll be good. I won't make a fuss. If you want to go away again tomorrow, I'll let you go. I promise. *(Starts to cry)* I can't help it. I don't want to cry. I can't stop myself . . . I know! The worst thing! You never could stand to have me cry. Taking such unfair advantage . . . What did she say? Was it good? Is that what she said? . . . Yes, it is. I heard her. Oh, my God! You mother-fucker! Shit-head! Fuck-face! Cunt! *(Throws the receiver down on to the floor)* Ah! Ah! Ah!

JOANNE *runs into the living room.*

RUTH *crawls on her hands and knees towards the telephone. She picks up the telephone and sits back on her heels.* RUTH *lifts the telephone above her head and smashes it down on to the floor.*

JOANNE: Jesus Christ!

RUTH *lunges at the coffee table. She sweeps the jumble of books and magazines on to the floor.*

JOANNE *takes hold of* RUTH *and tries to stop her from wrecking the whole apartment.* RUTH *struggles with* JOANNE, *ferociously, hitting out at her, wildly.* JOANNE *smothers the clumsy blows.*

JOANNE: What is it? Ruth! For God's sake!

RUTH: He was fucking her. Talking to me and fucking her . . . all the time he was talking . . .

JOANNE: Holy shit!

RUTH: I could hear. And she was laughing. He was telling her what I was saying to him and she was laughing. I told Steve all about . . . I told him what that man did to me . . . and he was . . . she was . . . ah! Ah! Ah!

The screams acquire a rhythmic and an almost insane pulse, as RUTH *loses what little control she still has over her emotions.*

JOANNE *holds* RUTH *by the shoulders and shakes her.* RUTH *rolls backwards and forwards, with the vigorous thrust and pull of* JOANNE'*s hands on her shoulders, until the screams choke in* RUTH'*s throat and her head lolls forward on to her chest.*

JOANNE *gathers* RUTH *into her arms and holds on to her, comforting her. She persuades* RUTH *to stand up and helps her to sit down on the sofa.*

JOANNE *sits beside* RUTH *and keeps her arms firmly around her.*

RUTH: I wanted to make him feel sorry for me. I shouldn't have gone walking by myself at night. I know that. I knew what could happen to me. I sort of hoped it would. If I was killed . . . I thought of that . . . I didn't care. Only, some way to make him feel responsible.

JOANNE: I know.

RUTH: It's not the first time. Nothing happened. I began to think it never would. No one even tried to pick me up.

JOANNE: Why didn't you talk to me?

RUTH: I couldn't talk to anyone. I haven't. Don't you know that? Since Steve left me, I haven't talked . . .

JOANNE: I thought . . . just me. For some reason I couldn't understand, you wouldn't talk . . .

RUTH: No one.

JOANNE: I'm glad to know that.

RUTH: I was so ashamed.

JOANNE: Because Steve left you?

RUTH: Yes.

JOANNE: Oh, baby!

RUTH: I didn't know what happened. Why it happened! And I only wanted him to come back home. On any terms! Humiliate myself! Oh, God! Six weeks after Steve walked out, I went to see him in his new apartment. I had no reason. I made no excuse. The girl was there with him. I just walked in and begged Steve to come back. I cried. I even went down on my knees. Can you believe that? What I put myself through! Trying to make that S.O.B. get back in bed . . . you know what I'm saying?

JOANNE: It's more than that. Don't sell yourself so cheap!

RUTH: That's where I miss him most. Not the making love. There got to be less and less the last two years. Having someone in the bed. I let the children sleep with me, when it gets too lonely. I'm sorry I went crazy. Did I wreck the 'phone?

JOANNE: I don't know. I haven't checked it out. *(Picks up the telephone. Puts the receiver to her ear.)* It doesn't seem to be working. Still, it's no great loss. I can't think of anyone who'd want to call me at this time of night.

RUTH *starts to cry.*

JOANNE: No one I'd want to talk to!

RUTH: I must stop crying. All this . . . is it . . . just, I want to kill myself and I don't have the nerve?

JOANNE: Do you want to kill yourself?

RUTH: Sometimes . . . if it wasn't for the children . . .

JOANNE: To punish Steve for walking out on you? Doesn't that make him more important than he is? More than anybody is!

RUTH: If I could believe he's really left me. We're divorced, I know, and everything . . . I can't accept . . .

JOANNE: How much of this is anything to do with Steve? You must not like yourself too much, if you lie down in garbage and let a man you don't know jerk off all over you. Steve didn't make you do that. It was your own idea.

RUTH: I didn't . . . let him . . .

JOANNE: You didn't stop him.

RUTH: He had the knife!

JOANNE: Where was the knife? While he was taking his prick out, did he put the knife away? What were you doing?

RUTH: He was sitting on me. I couldn't move.

JOANNE: Did you scream? How loud did you scream?

RUTH: He said . . . if I screamed . . . he'd cut my belly open.

JOANNE: If you set out to kill yourself . . . get yourself killed . . . you only had to struggle . . . scream!

RUTH: He cut my arm. He tried to cut my face.

JOANNE: He didn't cut your face.

RUTH: I thought . . . he'd kill me . . .

JOANNE: Did you want him to kill you?

RUTH: I wanted . . . Steve . . .

JOANNE: What . . . wanted Steve?

RUTH: If I was found dead and it was his fault . . .

JOANNE: Would he care?

RUTH: He'd never forgive himself.

JOANNE *laughs.*

JOANNE: Oh, baby! I'm sorry. I don't mean to laugh, but you don't know shit about your husband. He might go through the motions, for the benefit of friends, the family and the kids. Six months, he won't remember what you look like and the guilt, what guilt he might feel, maybe for the way you died . . . not the dying . . .

RUTH: What makes you so certain? You pretend to know so much about him. You don't even like Steve.

JOANNE: That's true. *(Laughing)* I can't stand him! I don't have the sort of difficulty you have when I think about him . . . I don't think about him! Only, some times, thinking about you.

RUTH: She was . . . and I was talking . . . he was laughing, telling her . . . and all the time . . .

JOANNE *puts her hand over* RUTH's *mouth, and for a moment, she stills the sound of her agony.*

Silence.

RUTH *brings her hand up and takes* JOANNE's *hand away from her mouth, interlinking fingers, holding on to the other woman's hand.*

RUTH: Why would he do that?

JOANNE: You don't know . . .

RUTH: Oh, yes.

JOANNE: Well, I knew a guy once had to call his wife, when he was fucking me. He couldn't get it up, he said, until he talked to her. She told him all the groceries she wanted him to buy, what the kids had done in school, the weather in Detroit! Nothing dirty. Nothing in the least bit sexy! It just turned him on to listen to her voice, while he was screwing me. My 'phone bill that year was fucking astronomical! *(Laughing)* Sorry about that! *(Disengages her hand from* RUTH's *hand.)* You can't guess why he'd let her fuck him and at the same time talk to you. I tried to understand it and I never could. Shit! What difference? He wasn't my husband. He was just an office trick. When I couldn't take it any more, I gave him the old heave-ho. *(Searches for a pack of cigarettes)* I found myself a guy who talked to me. Only, he was always asking, "Is it good? Is it the best? How is it for you, baby? Did you come yet?" Like he cared! Christ! You can go crazy . . . right? I want to know the fella's there. I can't keep telling him the whole time it's the best ride I ever had. Sometimes good, sometimes not so good. You have to know . . . the best of us . . . we have our bad days. If the ego can't accept a little criticism! I remember once, I told him, "Hey! What is it with the running commentary, Howard? Forget the words and get on with the fucking game!" Like I poured a bucket of cold water on him. I never saw a guy come down so quick. You've got to know that was the last time we were in the sack together. I still see him at the office and he makes a joke about it. "Hi, Joanne. Played any good games lately?" Like we know something no one else knows. Christ! I know something. He's an ass-hole and he has to tell himself he gets it on like God, each time he puts his prick inside some poor dumb cunt. Whatever! Maybe, it turns Stevie on. Gives him that magic sense of power. You got married to him. you tell me. What sort of kinky games did you play? Groping each other in the movies? Jerking him off in the Russian Tea Room? Fucking on the turnpike?

RUTH *shakes her head.*

JOANNE: That's the worst! Straight sex and water. Saving his best shot, all his guilty, secret fantasies for the women he can fuck and run away from. He has to see you every day. First thing in the morning, last thing at night and all the time between when he doesn't have the hots for anything more than eighteen holes of golf. Eighteen holes! Have you thought about that? Times I feel like a hole in the fucking ground! A fucking hole! You know what I'm telling you? What did you expect from Steve? You tell him a guy beat up on you. Tried to rape you! All those years old Stevie put it to you, did he ever once get a reaction out of you like that? Did you 'phone me and say, "Steve tried to rape me. Shit! Did that ever turn me on!" Did you ever tell him, "Sock it to me! Hose me, so I can't tell shit from applesauce!" Maybe, Steve wanted to rape you. Flip you over on your belly, tie you down and fuck the ass off you! Did you ask him, "Why do you need other women, when you've got more than you can handle here, right here, at home!" Did you ever get him to admit he had those other women?

RUTH *cries.*

JOANNE: Oh, baby!

JOANNE *sits on the sofa and puts her arms around* RUTH.

RUTH: . . . never did talk . . . never asked . . . I didn't have the courage . . .

JOANNE *rocks* RUTH, *gently.*

RUTH: . . . leave me, I thought, if I make a fuss. We didn't quarrel. When he left, I didn't make a scene . . .

RUTH *puts an arm around* JOANNE*'s back and leans against her.*

This is the first time RUTH *has made a physical movement towards* JOANNE.

RUTH: . . . never any argument. Steve always said, "We'll talk about it later, Ruth. It's not the time . . . " All the things I did to make him happy and content with me. I never made demands. It was always his decision, when we made love . . . (*Lifts her head off* JOANNE's *shoulder and looks up at her*) All that was wrong?

JOANNE: Whatever! He left you.

RUTH: I thought . . . just for a time. He will come back . . .

JOANNE: Baby.

JOANNE *kisses* RUTH, *softly, on the mouth.*

This gesture takes both women by surprise and they move slightly apart, as JOANNE *lifts her face away from* RUTH.

RUTH *does not withdraw completely from physical contact.* JOANNE's *arm rests on her shoulders and their hands lie together across* JOANNE's *lap.*

RUTH: You don't think he will come back?

JOANNE: I don't think that's the point. What Steve will do, that's something he knows. You can't anticipate . . .

RUTH: I always thought he would.

JOANNE: Do you still think so?

RUTH *shakes her head.*

JOANNE: Do you?

RUTH: No. I don't . . . think he will . . .

RUTH *starts to cry. She lunges incoherently into words and some scattered phrases.*

JOANNE *gathers* RUTH *into her arms.*

RUTH: . . . girl . . . the girl in bed . . . with Steve . . . young girl . . . did you talk to her? She's living there. Steve took her in. He's going to marry her.

JOANNE: You should feel sorry for the poor dumb cunt. She'll get the shaft. The same way you did.

RUTH: Steve introduced her to the children on the weekend. They're crazy about her.

JOANNE: What do they know? She gave them bubble gum and let them sit up to all hours, watching television. Kids! They'd sell each other for an extra scoop of ice cream.

RUTH: Steve wants me to let them stay with him for the holidays . . . Christmas and Summer . . . isn't that terrific? I can have them while they go to school. Do you believe that?

JOANNE: He came and told you . . .

RUTH: . . . took me out to lunch . . .

JOANNE: A class act, your ex-husband. Shit!

RUTH: When Steve left, he didn't want to see the children. And if he did, because I called and said they missed him. Most times, even then, he'd change his mind. He didn't care. And I had to tell them, disappoint them. They blamed me. They said I wouldn't let them see their father.

JOANNE: I should revise my opinion of old Stevie. I always said he was a first-class prick. I can see where he's in a class all by himself.

RUTH: I won't let him have the children.

JOANNE: Doesn't that hurt the children, Ruthie, more than it hurts Steve?

RUTH: It's not fair! *(The sudden violence is childlike and irrational.)*

JOANNE: You know it!

RUTH: Why should he . . . have her . . . and get the children, too. They only have a good time, when they stay with him. He doesn't make them tidy their rooms and brush their teeth, pick up their toys and do their homework. He doesn't have to send them off to bed in the middle of their favorite program, because it comes on too late and the school bus arrives at seven-thirty in the morning. They start to hate me.

JOANNE: No, they don't.

RUTH: They talk to me like I'm some kind of servant. And Maria, they treat her like a slave. I spend my life shouting at them and I never used to raise my voice. They're so mean to me. They never go to bed without an argument. The day can never end in peace. By the time I get rid of them, I'm so angry . . . they make me so angry . . .

JOANNE: *(Laughing)* Hey!

RUTH: Steve doesn't care. He doesn't try to discipline them, when they're with him. He wants the children to love him, so he lets them do just as they please.

JOANNE: They don't love him.

RUTH: They love him!

JOANNE: Not more than they love you.

RUTH: How can they love me? I'm the wicked witch, who screams at them all day and never lets them get away with anything. They'd go and live with Steve tomorrow, if they had any choice.

JOANNE: Ruthie, you can't spend your life in competition with a prick like Steve. He's always going to win. All the odds are on his side. He was never handsome. Getting older, he can only start to look less plain. And you know what they say, it doesn't matter to a woman what a fella looks like. You've got to know that's a rumor started by a really ugly guy!

In spite of herself, RUTH *laughs.*

JOANNE: Steve really did a job on you. Son-of-a-bitch! A gang of people want to fuck you, Ruth. If you didn't put on such a show of faithful wife, impregnable fortress, they'd be after you like fucking bears and honey. When you and Steve were still together, guys used to talk to me and speculate on what the chances were of getting you to fuck.

RUTH: Talk to you?

JOANNE: Oh, sure.

RUTH: Talk about me?

JOANNE: All the time.

RUTH: What did you tell them?

JOANNE: Ask her yourself.

RUTH: They never did.

JOANNE: They're not stupid. You're more faithful to the asshole now, than when you were married to him. Waiting for the Prodigal? Shit, Ruth! the worst thing Steve did wasn't leaving you. By that time, the damage was already done. Leaving, he just confirmed the things you felt about yourself, like, anyone who went to bed with you was doing you a favor ... right?

RUTH: I was never unfaithful.

JOANNE: I know that!

RUTH: I never wanted anyone but Steve.

JOANNE: I can't blame the S.O.B. for that. Your sickness has a far more ancient origin. When you were growing up, the highest aspiration ... right? Marriage, to a man a few years older, with a future full of promise and the serious intention of becoming a success.

RUTH: That's right.

JOANNE: That's wrong! They changed the rules. They told the guys it was OK for them to leave their wives and take off with the chicks they chase around all day at the office. Notice, they didn't tell you. They let you find out for yourself, by trial and error! I prefer a game with proper rules, like Monopoly. With cash penalties, and imprisonment, where you have to play according to instructions.

RUTH: I never thought it was deliberate. You make it seem like Steve set out to put me down. I don't think that's true.

JOANNE: Nothing personal? No, if he hadn't married you, it would have been some other poor cow.

RUTH: We had more good years than we had bad.

JOANNE: You want to get your photographs out and show me all the happy times you had together? Shit! If you don't know, Ruth, when you're better off!

RUTH: For a woman who never got married . . .

JOANNE: What does that tell you?

RUTH: . . . you make yourself out to be some kind of an expert!

JOANNE: When it comes to married men . . .

RUTH: I don't know what makes you think . . .

JOANNE: . . . I am an expert!

RUTH: . . . you can tell me anything . . .

JOANNE: I don't have to eat shit to know I wouldn't like it!

RUTH: The reason you never got married, Steve said, what kind of man would want a woman with bigger balls than him.

JOANNE: You made that up.

RUTH: Talks like a trucker, he said.

JOANNE: Steve?

RUTH: Fucks like a goat on estrogen!

JOANNE: Goddamn it, Ruth! You give yourself the right to say the first fucking thing comes into your empty head!

RUTH: One time, Steve said . . .

JOANNE: Do . . . whatever you believe . . .

RUTH: . . . you were after me.

JOANNE: . . . will help to get him back. (JOANNE *checks, momentarily, reacting to* RUTH'*s declaration and then, she plunges on, even more vehemently.*) What is that? Some kind of holy quest? In whose name? Christ! Why do you want him back? I fucked your husband. He's not much. There's a zebra in the San Diego Zoo who's got a prick five times the size, if size is what you're into. Maybe you're not much on animals. Though how you tell the difference . . . *(Silence)* The reason you don't have girl friends, don't you know? Steve fucks anything walks in the house and shows the least bit willing. I started fucking him about the time young Steve was born. What are you thinking?

RUTH *shakes her head.*

JOANNE: How much more of this . . .

RUTH: How long?

JOANNE: Three months. Not longer. The last time, he came by the office and he wanted me to fuck him on my desk. Well, he was drunk and Stevie always has an exaggerated notion of his sexual capacity, when he's been drinking. I decided it was time to call it quits. I've seen him, once in a while, we've fucked . . . not seriously . . . not since . . .

RUTH: How often did you see him?

JOANNE: The usual routine with your average married man. As often as possible the first couple of weeks, with every sort of crazy set-up and then, later . . . well, it settles down to twice a week. Eventually, you're lucky if you see him once as month. We had a weekend away together. You were out of town. After young Steve was born . . .

RUTH: I went to visit with my parents.

JOANNE: That's right.

RUTH: Were you with Steve the whole time I was away?

JOANNE: Jesus Christ! I couldn't spend that much time with God! No, just the weekend. Friday evening, we drove into Pennsylvania. Sunday, we came back. He spent the night.

RUTH: Steve didn't call me once that whole weekend. I thought . . . what's happened . . . I remember.

JOANNE: I've been trying to tell you ever since he left. I had the feeling you were getting more than your share of unexpected revelations. I don't have to ease my conscience. Not at your expense, anyway.

RUTH: Is that why . . . this apartment?

JOANNE: No.

RUTH: Did he come here? Did you . . . fuck . . .

JOANNE: What difference? He came to see me. Whatever! He didn't pay the rent.

RUTH: Did you . . . and Steve . . . *(Gestures awkwardly, at the bedroom)*

JOANNE: It had more to do with you, than wanting to make love to him. He's not that great in bed. He gets so involved with what he wants to do, there isn't time to deal with what's really happening. Didn't you find that?

RUTH *launches herself at* JOANNE, *with both arms stretched out in front of her. She crashes into* JOANNE *and drives her stumbling backwards.*

RUTH *swings one arm back, preparing to hit* JOANNE *in the face.* JOANNE *steps back, quickly and twists away from the furious onslaught.*

RUTH *catches hold of one of* JOANNE's *arms and wrenches at it, painfully, pulling* JOANNE *towards her.* RUTH *hits* JOANNE *in the chest.* JOANNE *breaks free and stumbles away, into a corner of the living room.*

RUTH *pursues* JOANNE, *implacably, with both arms out, clutching at her, as she backs up against the wall.* JOANNE *brings her arms up in front of her body and protects her face with her hands.*

RUTH *hits* JOANNE *on the arms with both hands.* JOANNE *hunches her shoulders and makes herself as small a target as she can. She does not respond to* RUTH'*s attack on her.*

RUTH *gasps audibly each time she swings an arm at* JOANNE. RUTH *starts to cry, making a harsh and childish sobbing. She slumps forward and falls against* JOANNE.

JOANNE *puts her arms around* RUTH *and supports the other woman, as she slips down, on to the floor.*

RUTH: Why did he? What do you know, more than I know? What did he want? I loved him. I told him he was the only man I wanted to make love with. He was the best, I told him. No one could make love like he could. Nights, when he came so quickly, I couldn't feel him in me, I wanted him to think I was satisfied. And I was! He made love to me. He wanted me, and if it satisfied him . . .

JOANNE: You don't have to do that.

RUTH: If he wanted something more from me, he didn't tell me. Why?

JOANNE: You're his wife. And if there have been other men, when you married him, they're forgotten. Like . . . instant virgin! You're not supposed to come on like a whore.

RUTH: You can?

JOANNE: He treats me like a whore. I behave like one. He uses me. I let him. I'm using him, I tell myself. Christ! You don't ever use a man. He puts it to you, leaves himself in you, and takes nothing with him, when he walks away.

RUTH: Did I hurt you?

JOANNE: Yes.

RUTH: I'm sorry.

JOANNE: No, you're not.

RUTH: *(Laughing)* No, I'm not.

JOANNE: Damn right!

RUTH: Why did you tell me?

JOANNE: I was angry. Shit! With all that stuff? What do you expect? It makes quite a picture. You and Steve, in bed together, making jokes!

RUTH: We weren't in bed.

JOANNE: Whatever. I went crazy. You can understand?

RUTH: I can understand.

JOANNE: I wanted to tell you.

RUTH: While it was going on?

JOANNE: No.

RUTH: When it was over.

JOANNE: Making love to Steve, I thought, I might get closer. I don't know. That could be a rationalization of some real intention to make you eat shit. I take my full share of responsibility. More, perhaps, I often had the feeling Steve was just a bit surprised how easily he got me into bed.

RUTH: Sleeping with my husband! That's going to bring us closer together?

JOANNE: Bring me . . . closer to you . . .

RUTH: And telling me about it?

JOANNE: A risk I had to take. One day, I've always known, I'd have to tell you.

RUTH: Why? No one else is going to. Certainly not Steve! Who else knows?

JOANNE: It doesn't matter who else knows! Shit! No one else. I know! If you want to leave, because you know I fucked your husband, well, what's stopping you? If you want to stay, in spite of knowing, and that's the worst there is to know. In my opinion, anyway, the very worst! If we can like ourselves enough to love each other, and there's nothing we have to be ashamed of, if we're going to try, Ruth, be together, then there can't be any shame.

RUTH: Does it make things better? Telling me?

JOANNE: Yes. If you won't take fright and run away.

RUTH: It still happened. You and Steve. Nothing alters that.

JOANNE: Maybe not. But it isn't a secret any more. Something despicable, between me and your ex-husband.

RUTH: As long as we can't change the past, I don't see the sense pretending anything can be different. Things happen to people and you can't talk about them. You can't absolve me. I don't want absolution! In the end, nothing's changed, and if I can't forgive myself, then telling you won't help me.

JOANNE: Bullshit! Telling me may be your only shot! You've already told me more about yourself than you've told anyone before. I know you, Ruth. You don't tell shit! Hide it away inside and smile a lot. For your own sake, for mine, baby, talk it out.

RUTH: . . . don't want to . . .

JOANNE: *(Laughing)* The hell you don't!

RUTH: I don't want to tell you bad things!

JOANNE: Whatever!

RUTH: You don't know.

JOANNE: Try me. Trust me.

RUTH . . . shame . . .

JOANNE: How did you meet him in the first place? Where?

RUTH: . . . coffee shop . . . colder out than I expected . . . only had my lighter coat on . . . sitting at the counter . . . don't know how long . . .

JOANNE *leads* RUTH, *cautiously, towards her confession.*

JOANNE: He spoke to you?

RUTH: No.

JOANNE: He was looking at you?

RUTH: Yes. He smiled. I didn't think he was smiling at me. I thought . . . someone . . . maybe sitting next to me. It wasn't any sort of smile . . .

JOANNE: He paid his check and left? Did you follow him?

RUTH: No.

JOANNE: He was waiting for you?

RUTH: It was late and I told Maria . . . started home . . . in the alley, on the far side of the street, watching me . . . I think . . . waiting for me . . .

JOANNE: You went over to him?

RUTH: I wasn't frightened . . . walked across the street . . . didn't see . . . I was looking at his face . . . I didn't see his . . . thing . . . his penis . . . he had taken his penis out and he was holding it.

JOANNE: Oh, baby.

RUTH: It was beautiful. White and big . . . I thought . . . huge . . . and he was smiling. I walked into the alley. I was shaking . . . and my voice . . . I tried to speak to him. I couldn't make the words right.

JOANNE: He got hold of you?

RUTH: . . . hands on my shoulders . . . pushed me down on to my knees in front of him . . . rubbed his penis up against my mouth. He said, "Open your mouth up, cunt! You know what to do. Get on with it and easy with the teeth."

JOANNE: You tried to get away?

RUTH: I hit him. I wanted to scream. He put his hands around my throat. He said, "Bitch!" and "What the fuck you think you're doing?" His penis wasn't big now. It was hanging down. He let go of me and covered it with his hand. "Cock-sucker," he said, and he hit me. I fell backwards. There were trash cans . . . knocked them over and the garbage spilled out. He rolled me over on my stomach and he . . . urinated on me . . .

RUTH *brings her hands up to her face and smells them.*

JOANNE: There's nothing, Ruthie. There's no smell . . .

RUTH: . . . pulled me up on to my feet . . . threw me back against the wall . . . he said, "You're going to get it now." He had a knife. He jammed the point against my stomach and he said, "You come looking for it, lady, and you're going to get it!"

JOANNE: Son-of-a-bitch!

RUTH: . . . hit him in the face . . . shouted and hit him . . . kept on hitting him and screaming, I remember . . . tried to cut my face . . . I put my arms up . . . hit me in the stomach with his fist . . .

JOANNE *starts to cry.*

RUTH: . . . lying on the ground and he was sitting on me, leaning over me, and with the knife against my face. He said, "This time, lady, or I'll cut your face. I'll slit your belly open, if you don't do it right this time." His penis was big again and he was holding it. I opened my mouth and I let him put his penis into me. I wanted him to. I would have . . . the first time . . . if he hadn't hurt me. I knew what he wanted from me, when I walked into the alley, and he knew . . . if he hadn't spoken to me . . . called me . . .

Silence.

RUTH: He was on his hands and knees. He was hurting me. I tried to pull my head back and he said, "Hey, baby! What're you doing? Daddy got himself a prick too big for you to swallow? Shit! I'm not halfway in there. Don't you know? You've got to open wide for Daddy!" And he put his fingers in my mouth. He held it open and rammed his penis into me. "Oh, God!" he said. "I'm going to come."

JOANNE *put one hand over her stomach and the other hand on her stomach.*

JOANNE: Ah!

RUTH: He put his hand behind my head and pulled it up towards him. He kept his penis still now and he jerked my head about, backwards and forwards. He was making little whining sounds and when he came, he shouted. I couldn't swallow all of it. I coughed, and retched, and there was more, and I threw up. He got off me quickly, and he laughed. He said, "When Daddy fucks you, baby, you know you've been fucked!" He wiped his hands off and his penis on my coat.

JOANNE *shakes her head and covers her mouth with both hands.*

RUTH: "Baby, I'll be looking out for you," he said. "Next time, you won't have to play so hard to get. Next time, we can both of us have a good time." He held his knife in front of my face and he said, "Don't forget. You talk to anybody and I'll have to cut you up. I wouldn't like to do that," he said, and he went away.

Silence.

RUTH: I didn't want him to come so quickly. I wanted him to go on fucking me. I wanted . . . more . . . and his penis!

Silence.

RUTH: It wasn't just to make Steve feel guilty, and come back to me.

JOANNE: I forgot old Stevie. No, I can dig it.

RUTH: Whatever he wanted to do . . . whatever he did . . .

JOANNE: Write it down! You'll sell a million copies! Shit! I'd like to meet the guy myself. Sounds like he can really put it to you. *(Gently)* What am I going to say? I love you. Is there any more you have to tell me?

RUTH *shakes her head.*

JOANNE: *(Laughing)* Thank Christ for that! Hey! You want to tell me you're ashamed? I know that. You dug this guy giving it to you in some alley, after he pissed all over you. Okay. You should be ashamed. Don't make a habit of it. You might not be so lucky next time. Say fifteen 'Hail Marys,' and put twenty dollars in the plate. Listen, if you want to talk it out again, with some added details, I can dig it. I won't like it. I'll tell you that up front.

RUTH: I want to forget . . .

JOANNE: I'm glad you said that. I thought maybe you were going to work it up and do it as a number, when you go to parties.

RUTH *puts a hand up to her face and smells it.*

JOANNE: You must stop doing that. You know that? I'm going to soak you in disinfectant, scrub you down with Borax and then hang you out to dry. I won't let you back inside until the worst thing you can smell is rose oil, incense and perfume. Hey! Why don't you take a shower? Nothing personal! I love the way you don't smell. You're not going home tonight. You're staying here with me.

RUTH: I don't want to go.

JOANNE: I won't let you.

RUTH *starts to shake.*

JOANNE *puts her arms around* RUTH *and holds on to her, tightly.*

JOANNE: 'Kay. Okay. Relax. You're safe here. I won't let anyone come in and get you. You're with me.

RUTH: I will forget.

JOANNE: I guarantee.

RUTH: I can still . . . taste . . .

JOANNE *kisses* RUTH *on the lips.*

Silence.

JOANNE: You get yourself undressed. I'll turn the shower on. Unless you'd rather have a bath?

RUTH *shakes her head.*

JOANNE *takes* RUTH *into the bedroom*

The buzzer sounds.

JOANNE *walks into the living room and throws a pillow, sheets and a blanket on to the sofa.*

RUTH *steps into the bedroom doorway.*

RUTH: I won't be long.

JOANNE: Take all the time you want.

RUTH: You're not going to sleep in here?

JOANNE: Whatever.

RUTH: I don't want to sleep by myself.

JOANNE: You got it.

RUTH *walks into the bedroom.*

The buzzer sounds again.

JOANNE *searches through the jumble on one of the bookshelves, looking for a pack of cigarettes.*

JOANNE *switches off one of the table lamps. She finds a pack of cigarettes and switches off the other lamp. She leaves the living room in darkness and walks into the bedroom.*

The buzzer sounds again.

[END OF ACT ONE]

Act Two

Night.

*J*OANNE *and* R*UTH *are entertaining dinner guests in* J*OANNE'*s *apartment.*

Dinner is finished and the two men, M*IKE *and* W*ALLY *have moved away from the table. They are smoking marijuana, sharing the hand-made cigarette between them.*

M*IKE *is on his feet and talking, as he walks around the living room.* W*ALLY *is sitting on the couch and drifting, in a peaceful haze of goodwill.*

J*OANNE *is sitting at the dinner table. The remains of the meal have not been cleared away.* J*OANNE *has a cup of coffee on the table, in front of her. She is wearing a caftan. Her hair is loose and falls around her shoulders.*

R*UTH *is sitting in an armchair. She is wearing a kimono. The patterned silk, tied around the waist, moulds itself to the shape of her body. Her hair is loose and frames her face, with a golden radiance, which is heightened by the glow from the lamp, on the table, beside the armchair.*

MIKE: "Life is a fountain." And the guy said, "Shit!"

WALLY: Hey!

W*ALLY *is startled into momentary and unwelcome awareness by* M*IKE'*s *use of the four-letter word.*

MIKE: Right. *(Gives the cigarette to* WALLY*)* He said, "What is that! You know how long it took me, getting here? You know what it cost? I went to Harvard. Post-graduate at Oxford, and I asked my professor, "What is the meaning of life?" And he said, "My boy, I can't tell you. I don't know. But there is a man. He teaches in Vienna. Maybe, he can tell you." I went to Vienna and I studied with the guy, and he said, "Meaning? You want to know meaning? What . . . meaning? What!" *(Takes the cigarette from* WALLY, *who is giggling childishly at* MIKE'S *caricature of the make-believe Jewish idiom.)* He said, "There is only one man. He is a lama, in Tibet. Ask him. He can tell you." I worked twenty years. I saved money for the expedition. I climbed the goddamn mountains. You know how many people died, on the way up here? Do you want to know! Three men died, and I lost three more, fatally injured. I'm the only one to survive, and all you can tell me, "Life is a fountain! What is that shit!" And the lama said, "Life isn't a fountain."

WALLY *starts to laugh before* MIKE *delivers the punch line. He laughs through the end of the story and on, sitting forward and choking.*

JOANNE: You want some coffee, Ruth?

WALLY: Funny. That's a funny bit!

JOANNE: It's not that funny.

WALLY: Jesus!

MIKE: Always gets him like that.

JOANNE: Must be why you keep him around.

MIKE: You're not smoking.

JOANNE: Shall I make some fresh?

RUTH: No, thanks. Not for me.

MIKE *offers the cigarette to* RUTH.

RUTH: I don't smoke.

MIKE: It's not the same. It isn't exactly smoking. Here.

JOANNE: She doesn't have to, if she doesn't want to. Why should she?

RUTH: I never have.

MIKE: You don't know what you're missing. Doesn't know what she's missing, Wally. Right?

WALLY: Right!

JOANNE: You don't have to.

RUTH: Oh, sure. Why not?

RUTH *takes the cigarette and places it, cautiously, between her lips, in the center of her mouth. She tries to draw smoke into her mouth and when she succeeds in doing so, she starts to cough.*

MIKE *and* WALLY *laugh at her.*

JOANNE: Give it to me. (*Holds the cigarette between her finger tips and draws smoke into her mouth and then deep into her lungs.*)

RUTH: Doesn't it burn you?

MIKE: You get used to it.

RUTH: I don't think so.

MIKE: Give it time. Get used to anything, in time.

JOANNE: The reason it makes you cough, it's got to be the worst damn stuff I ever poked. Shit, Mike! Where did you get this?

JOANNE *gives the cigarette to* MIKE.

MIKE *cannot mask his momentary discomfort, when* JOANNE *uses the four-letter word.*

JOANNE: Does that upset you? I'm not supposed to say naughty words? What should I say? Shoot? or, sugar? My mother used to say, "Sugar!" Any time she got uptight. Isn't that sort of cute?

RUTH: Should I feel something?

JOANNE: With that stuff, you wouldn't feel lightning, if it hit you in the ass! Nobody wants any coffee?

MIKE: You've had a lot of experience?

JOANNE: Majored in pot. Took coke, as a minor. Sure, I've had experience. What do you want to know?

MIKE: Where can I get some of the better stuff?

JOANNE: You don't want to fool around. If that turns you on, the stuff I use will really blow you out.

MIKE *laughs, an instinctive, masculine response, which* MIKE *uses to mask any feeling of insecurity.*

JOANNE: You want to do your party piece now? Have you got a joke you want to tell us?

WALLY: No.

JOANNE: Can't sit around in silence. Got to keep the party going! Hey! Why don't we play pornographic proverbs?

WALLY: I hate party games.

JOANNE: It's simple. Anyone can play.

MIKE: You want to give us an example?

JOANNE: A blow-joy a day, keeps the doctor out-of-sight!

MIKE: There's more than one way to screw a cat.

JOANNE: Ruthie?

RUTH: No!

JOANNE: Taking the bull by the balls.

MIKE: Every cunt has a silver lining.

JOANNE: All that glistens, isn't vaseline.

MIKE: The longer you wait . . .

JOANNE: The harder it gets!

MIKE: Score half a point each on that one.

JOANNE: You can lead a horse to shit, but you can't make him eat.

MIKE: It's an ill wind . . . and blowing . . . something! Come on, Wally!

JOANNE: No, you're disqualified. We've already had a blow-job.

MIKE: Speak for yourself.

RUTH: All cats look grey in the dark.

MIKE: No good. We've had a cat.

WALLY: Anyway, it isn't pornographic.

JOANNE: Why don't I tell a joke? The bell rang in this brothel, and the Madame opened the door. There was a fellow on the stoop, and he was lying in a basket. He had no arms and no legs, and the Madame said, "What do you want?" The man said, "What else? I want to get laid." The Madame said, "For Christ's sake! How?" So the fellow said, "I rang the doorbell, didn't I"

The men's response to the joke is minimal, a masculine reaction to a dirty joke, when it is told by a woman.

JOANNE: You had to be there.

RUTH: I think it's funny.

JOANNE: I'll try another. This guy was telling his friend how he couldn't make out, and his friend said to him, "Right! And you never will, until you learn to treat them better. It's just the one thing with you, all the time, and they don't take to that. You have to give them dinner. Talk to them. Make them feel like they're intelligent. Like it isn't only sex!" And the guy said, "Talk to them? What about?" His friend said, "Talk about the movies. Books you've read. The theater." So the guy takes this chick out and he says to her, "You know Shakespeare?" And the chick says, "Yes . . . "

MIKE: And the guy says, "Okay. Let's fuck!"

JOANNE: I always wondered who the guy was. Shit! Don't you hate those stories, where they change the names, to protect the guilty. You want to hear some music?

MIKE: Whatever you're on, it's doing more for you, than this stuff does for me.

JOANNE: I told you, Mike. You've got really bad shit there.

MIKE: You want to share your good stuff with me?

JOANNE: You want to get down to business? What you guys have been thinking about all evening? You want to tell us? Better yet! Why don't we get into it, and see what goes down?

MIKE: You're flying a whole different pattern, Jo!

JOANNE: Don't you want to fuck? Wally, don't you?

MIKE: Is that what you're talking about?

JOANNE: Do we have to play games?

MIKE: 'Scuse me!

JOANNE: We're not kids.

MIKE: Right!

JOANNE: I'm not about to be surprised, when you send Wally home with Ruth, and stay behind yourself to help me with the dishes. It was you feeling me up during dinner? I know it wasn't Ruth and Wally was sitting on the other side.

MIKE: You don't fool around!

JOANNE: On the contrary . . .

WALLY: I don't want to take Ruth home.

JOANNE: Does it embarrass you, Wally?

WALLY: I'm sorry. I don't mean . . .

RUTH: I know what you mean.

MIKE: Always got to be a first time, I guess.

WALLY: It's only ten o'clock.

JOANNE: What else are we going to do? You want to talk about the economic situation and the possibility of another recession, unemployment and devaluation? I know less about that than you do. Why don't we go to bed? You want to get your rocks off? Isn't it possible I feel the same way and can't we talk, as if it's something we can enjoy, and not a cross between bad breath and body odor, something we have to whisper?

MIKE: Who's whispering?

JOANNE: Which one of us? Given you had a choice?

MIKE: Do I?

JOANNE: Up to a point.

MIKE: 'Kay. (*Puts his arm around* JOANNE'*s shoulders, proprietorially*) Time to go, Wally.

WALLY: We just finished eating.

MIKE: What do you think? You'll get stomach cramps?

WALLY: I don't see why we have to rush.

JOANNE: Don't you want to get home, Wally? What time is your train?

WALLY: I'm not taking the train.

JOANNE: Are you driving? Is that why you're not drinking?

WALLY: I'm staying in town overnight.

JOANNE: That's convenient. Isn't that convenient, Ruthie?

MIKE: Wally, will you get Ruthie's coat?

WALLY: I'd like some more coffee.

MIKE: Shit!

JOANNE: Nobody's gong to change their mind, Mike, and play hard to get. If that's what you're worrying about? Come on. Sit down and have another drink.

RUTH: Why don't I make the coffee?

JOANNE: Why don't I?

RUTH: I can't think of one good reason.

For the first time, it is apparent that the two women are playing a game, which they have set up, before the two men arrived.

JOANNE: Will you make a drink for Mike? *(Pats* MIKE *on the bottom as she walks into the kitchen)*

MIKE: Scotch. On the rocks.

RUTH: I'll have to get some ice. *(Follows* JOANNE *into the kitchen)*

MIKE: Will you get out of here!

WALLY: Mike! For Christ's sake!

MIKE: What's wrong with you? You don't like Ruth?

WALLY: I like her.

MIKE: Right!

WALLY: Maybe I don't want to get laid.

MIKE: What does she have to do? Open your fly and take it out? She's done everything else.

WALLY: Joanne . . .

MIKE: Listen to me, Wally . . .

WALLY: I'm not sure Ruth . . .

MIKE: . . . and hear me good! The guys at the office have been telling me about Joanne and what a great lay! I've been trying to get next to her for six fucking months and now, she's coming at me, with her legs wide open. Shit! You get your ass out of here, Wally.

WALLY: What am I going to do with Ruth? I can't take her back to the hotel.

MIKE: Why not? Why can't you?

WALLY: They know me.

MIKE: Shit!

WALLY: And my wife has stayed there.

MIKE: Why couldn't you stay somewhere they didn't know you? Ass-hole!

WALLY: Hey!

MIKE: 'Kay! Okay! The way they've got this all set up, more than likely, she'll take you home with her.

WALLY: Where do you get off . . .

MIKE: Look, don't worry. Play it by ear.

WALLY: Don't call me ass-hole!

MIKE: I'm sorry.

WALLY: One thing I can tell you about Joanne. She'll break your balls.

MIKE: If I get really lucky.

RUTH *walks out of the kitchen.*

RUTH: If you want ice, you'll have to wait, I'm afraid. We're out of ice.

MIKE: No problem. You can forget the drink.

JOANNE *walks out of the kitchen.*

MIKE: It's getting sort of late, and Wally . . .

WALLY: I've got an early start tomorrow.

MIKE: He's changed his mind about staying on.

JOANNE: I just got through fixing the coffee.

WALLY: I'll get your coat, Ruth.

JOANNE: Why?

MIKE: Wally's going to take Ruthie home.

JOANNE: No, no!

MIKE: Shit!

JOANNE: Did I say anything about Ruthie going home with Wally? Ruth, did you?

RUTH: No, I didn't.

MIKE: 'Kay. Okay.

JOANNE: What gave you the idea . . .

MIKE: I'll have that drink now.

JOANNE: Why don't you make up your mind?

MIKE: *(Anger)* Why don't you?

JOANNE: *(Laughing)* Hey!

MIKE: You said we weren't going to play games. Right?

JOANNE: I'm not playing games.

MIKE: You want us to beg for it?

JOANNE: Whatever turns you on!

MIKE: Get us feeling horny, and then, keep us all strung out?

JOANNE: If you're feeling horny, Mike, what are we doing, standing here and talking about it?

MIKE: What else are we going to do?

JOANNE: Use your imagination.

MIKE: Honey, I gave up jerking off when my divorce came through.

JOANNE: There's more than one room to the apartment. Wally and Ruth can entertain themselves in here . . .

MIKE: And we go into the bedroom?

JOANNE: Unless Wally wants to go first, with Ruth? If he's in such a hurry . . .

MIKE: He isn't.

WALLY: You're not serious?

MIKE: Yes, she is.

WALLY: I'm going. I'm not staying here.

RUTH: Please don't go. Stay and keep me company.

MIKE: Don't worry, Wally. You'll get yours.

JOANNE: Smoke a little. Have a drink. Relax.

MIKE *puts his arm around* JOANNE*'s waist.*

MIKE: Ready when you are.

JOANNE: I hope so.

JOANNE *takes* MIKE *into the bedroom.*

RUTH: Would you like some coffee?

WALLY: If it's not a lot of trouble?

MIKE: Hey there, Jo! Take it easy!

RUTH: Why don't I close the door?

WALLY *mumbles an inaudible reply and shrugs his shoulders.*

RUTH *closes the door.*

WALLY: . . . don't believe . . .

RUTH: What did you say?

WALLY: I don't believe any of this! I had no idea . . .

RUTH: You did expect to end up in bed with me?

WALLY: I don't know you. I never met you before!

RUTH: What difference does that make? Mike brought you along for the ride. He certainly expected Joanne to go to bed with him.

WALLY: Maybe. I don't know.

MIKE: What did he tell you about Joanne?

WALLY: They work in the same office.

RUTH: Is that all?

WALLY: He wants to sleep with her.

RUTH: What did he say about me?

WALLY: What could he say? More than you're a friend of Joanne. That's all he knows about you.

RUTH: He didn't tell you I'm divorced?

WALLY: Yes, he told me that.

RUTH: What else?

WALLY: Nothing else!

RUTH: Mike seemed to expect I'd go to bed with you. I got the impression he was pretty confident.

WALLY: I don't give a damn what Mike expects.

RUTH: What do you expect? Why did you come here with Mike?

WALLY: Joanne invited him to dinner, and she said . . .

RUTH: Bring a friend for Ruth?

WALLY: That's right.

RUTH: Why did you decide to stay in town?

WALLY: I've got a meeting. First thing in the morning. It's a drag, getting all the way home and back again.

RUTH: You can get home and back?

WALLY: If I want to spend half my life on a train!

RUTH: Where do you stay, when you spend the night in town?

WALLY: I take a room in a hotel.

RUTH: You don't have an apartment?

WALLY: No, I don't have an apartment. I can't afford to keep an apartment for the one or two nights every month I spend in town.

RUTH: You don't stay in town more than that?

WALLY: I don't stay, unless I absolutely have to.

RUTH: And tonight?

Silence.

WALLY *walks into the kitchen.*

The sound of JOANNE, *responding to* MIKE, *as he makes love to her. One cry, hardly heard, and not repeated.*

RUTH *switches on the hi-fi and sorts through the cassettes.*

WALLY *walks out of the kitchen. He is carrying a cup of coffee.*

WALLY: I'm sorry.

RUTH: You don't have to apologize.

WALLY: I didn't ask. Would you like some coffee?

RUTH: Oh. No, thanks.

RUTH *puts a cassette into the tape deck and presses the "play" button. She sets the volume at a background level.*

WALLY: I don't know what I'm doing here.

RUTH: Bullshit! The same as Mike. Sniffing after Joanne. Looking for freebies. A piece of ass you don't have to pay for. Maybe, if she's a good lay, something you can have again, on a semi-permanent basis, which won't interfere too much with your daily routine and might help to bolster the sagging ego of a middle-aging man, with nothing to look forward to, except another ten years, sitting at the same desk, signing the same order forms, and making out the same expense sheet.

WALLY: How old do you think I am?

RUTH: Forty-seven. Forty-eight.

WALLY: I'm forty-five!

RUTH: Is that the only thing you heard?

WALLY: I figure on more than ten years.

RUTH: By the time you get to fifty-five, they'll be throwing younger men than you on to the scrap heap.

The sound of JOANNE, *responding passionately, a louder cry, more sustained.*

Neither RUTH, *nor* WALLY, *can pretend they have not heard the cry, and equally, neither one can admit to the other that they have.*

WALLY: I came here because Mike told me I couldn't miss. You're right. I stayed in town because I don't want to get home late, and have to tell lies to my wife.

RUTH: Suppose I want you to stay the night?

WALLY: I thought about that.

RUTH: Your wife might 'phone the hotel.

WALLY: Only in a crisis.

RUTH: They do happen.

WALLY: Sometimes you have to gamble.

The sound of JOANNE, *responding uninhibitedly.*

WALLY: Why don't I take you home?

RUTH: I've got three children and a nanny waiting for me at home. The children don't like waking up and finding strangers sleeping in their Mommy's bed. You can't take me home. Unless you've decided you don't want to fuck?

WALLY *reacts to* RUTH's *deliberate use of the four-letter word.*

He has adjusted to JOANNE's *casual use of obscenities and accepted* RUTH's *capacity for direct statement. The combination of them both, and in* RUTH's *mouth, still takes him by surprise.*

RUTH: We don't have to. There's no obligation. I can see, if you don't get Joanne, you might feel, second best.

WALLY: Oh, no.

RUTH: No. I don't think so either.

WALLY: It's not that.

RUTH: Just the same, I could understand . . .

WALLY: I can't stay here. Can you? With Mike . . . and Joanne!

RUTH: Much like visiting a brothel, I imagine. Only they have more rooms, and you don't have to wait.

WALLY: We can go to my hotel.

RUTH: Does it bother you? Waiting? What happens as a general rule? Straight in, straight at it, and straight out again?

WALLY: I don't go to brothels.

RUTH: Aren't brothels rather old-fashioned, anyway? Don't they have out-calls now? A visiting masseuse? Like sending out for coffee and a doughnut. We deliver to your door!

WALLY: Mike said you set this whole thing up.

RUTH: If you don't want to fuck me, you don't have to hang around.

WALLY: He said you're both desperate to get laid.

RUTH: Looks like I wasted my share of a perfectly good dinner, and a better than ordinary wine.

WALLY: You don't have any right to put me down.

RUTH: I don't aim to.

WALLY: If you want me to get out . . .

RUTH: What makes you think . . .

WALLY: Goddamn it! Don't treat me like a dirty-minded little boy!

RUTH: Don't treat me like a cunt.

WALLY: If you behave like a whore . . .

RUTH: If you act like a trick! Take your hand out of your pocket, it won't get any bigger.

WALLY: I didn't come here . . .

RUTH: I don't care why you came here, Wally. If you can't get off any more, fucking your wife, that's your problem. I don't want to hear about it. If she believes in making children, every time she fucks, talk to Family Planning. If she won't fuck, talk to your analyst. Talk to her analyst! Maybe she's fucking him, and he can tell you how to turn her on. Whatever! Right? I can't get into that. As long as we both know, we don't exist for each other, outside this room and the bedroom, we don't exist! You can't take me home. I don't go to your hotel. Here, or nowhere, nothing! Got it? Have you got it? Do you understand?

Silence.

RUTH: *(Laughing)* Say something, Wally. If it's only goodbye.

WALLY: You don't know shit about my wife.

RUTH: I don't want to.

WALLY: I won't talk about my wife.

RUTH: Poor bitch!

WALLY: What makes you think you're so much better?

RUTH: I don't think I am.

WALLY: Because I'm here . . . right? You want to know why I'm here?

RUTH *starts to laugh.*

WALLY: Joanne puts out for every other guy in the office. Mike figured it was his turn, and if she puts out, you've got to know her girl friend's more of the same. Freebies? Right!

Fucking freebies! I just hope it's worth the static. You want to play this game, you have to know when you're supposed to keep your mouth shut. Maybe it's the waiting? Makes you nervous? We don't have to wait. What's wrong with the sofa? We don't need a bed. There's always the floor. You've had it on the floor? We don't have to take our clothes off, if you're scared they'll come in and catch us at it? What have you got on, anyway? It doesn't look like you're wearing anything at all under that . . . kimono? Is that what it is? Come here. You talk a great game. What's the action like? Come here!

RUTH *shakes her head.*

WALLY: You want me chasing after you? You do like to play games. What's wrong, Ruthie? Frightens you, does it? Turns you on? What does turn you on? Shit! You want me to beat up on you? I'll tell you, more than once, lady, you've come close. Another guy, he might have punched you out. Would you like that? What is it about you makes me want to hurt you? You talk dirty, like you know where it's at. I've got to tell you, I'm not convinced. The way you talk, the way you act, you know? Like a bad impersonation of your ball-breaking friend.

The sound of JOANNE, *moaning, in rhythmic response to* MIKE.

WALLY: Hear that? Do you hear that? You want a piece of what Mike is giving her? I'll make you shout. I'll make you scream. I'll fuck you, lady. I'll have your ass!

RUTH *loses all sense of where she is.*

As WALLY *walks towards her, reaching to take hold of her, with both hands,* RUTH *turns to run and takes a short step, walking straight into the wall, which is immediately behind her.*

RUTH *knocks the breath out of her body, but more than the physical shock of the collision, the emotional shock of walking blindly into the wall, sends her staggering sideways. She stumbles into a chair and knocks it over.*

WALLY *laughs, momentarily startled, as* RUTH *walks into the wall, and then, he catches his breath, appalled by the consequences of the act and afraid to help, knowing he began the series of accidents.*

JOANNE: *(Calling)* Ruthie? Are you all right? Ruthie!

RUTH: I'm all right.

RUTH'*s response is automatic. It is not necessarily truthful.*

JOANNE: *(Calling)* What's going on?

RUTH: Nothing.

JOANNE: *(Calling)* Wally?

WALLY: She's all right. *(Awkwardly)* Are you?

RUTH: Yes.

WALLY: You scared me. What were you thinking? Christ! Where were you?

RUTH: You scared me!

WALLY: I thought you'd gone crazy. I mean, what is that, running into a wall!

RUTH: Pretty funny.

WALLY: Well, yes. In a way.

RUTH: I can imagine.

WALLY: I'm sorry, if I scared you.

RUTH: The last thing I remember, you were trying to get hold of me. I thought, he wants to kill me.

WALLY: You're not serious?

RUTH: Why?

WALLY: Something to do with them, the two of them, in there. And Joanne, making all that noise.

RUTH: Nothing to do with me?

WALLY: What was all that stuff about my wife? You don't know anything about us and the way we live.

RUTH: She lets you spend the night in town. That tells me something.

WALLY: We don't live in each other's pockets.

RUTH: Will you 'phone, when you get back to the hotel? Will you talk to her tonight?

WALLY: Maybe. I don't know.

RUTH: Is she waiting up? Hoping you'll call? Worried, if you don't? Does she know why you want to stay in town? Is she understanding?

WALLY: We live out there, because she wants to.

RUTH: Yes, of course.

WALLY: You can't bring up children in the city.

RUTH: The children!

WALLY: No place where they can ride their bikes. No place to run and play. There's always danger in the city. If it isn't traffic, it's the guys who hang out in the parks.

RUTH: How many children?

WALLY: Three boys.

RUTH: How old are they?

WALLY: Danny, the oldest boy, he's seventeen. How old are your kids?

RUTH: I don't want to talk about my children. What about the other two?

WALLY: Fifteen, and seven.

RUTH: Seven? That's like starting over.

WALLY: I guess . . .

RUTH: She's got plenty of company around the house. Never lonely.

WALLY: Never gets a minute to herself.

RUTH: She says.

JOANNE's *rhythmic response to* MIKE *becomes more insistent, as she comes towards her climax.*

WALLY: There she goes! Makes you feel you're missing out on something good, the way she carries on.

RUTH: Turn up the music, if it bothers you.

WALLY: It doesn't bother me. *(Sits forward and lowers his voice to a furtive, almost conspiratorial level, as he tells the story)* One night, I was staying in a hotel. Somewhere. I forget. And this couple in the next room, they were screwing half the night. I got off just lying there and listening to them do it.

RUTH: You were on your own?

WALLY: What? Oh, sure! On my own! Did you ever calculate how many nights you spend on your own, when you could be with someone? What's to stop you? Aren't there plenty of other people on their own, and wouldn't they be happy, getting together? More than happy! It drives me crazy, when I'm on my own, and there's no reason why I should be . . . just . . .

RUTH: There's no reason.

WALLY: Doesn't a man owe something to the woman, who has his children? Loyalty . . .

JOANNE *reaches her climax and cries out, wildly.*

WALLY: Christ! Mike is really putting it to her. Will you listen? I never heard anyone . . .

RUTH *turns up the volume of the music.*

WALLY: Too late. If I'm any judge . . .

Ruth *hits the "stop" button and the music breaks off, in mid-phrase.*

WALLY: Do you make a lot of noise?

RUTH: I don't know. I never listen. Why? Will it embarrass you, if I do?

WALLY: Things don't embarrass me. You keep asking . . .

RUTH: Yes. Maybe I'm more easily embarrassed than I think.

WALLY: If we're going through with this . . .

WALLY: What else have you been waiting for?

WALLY: You're not scared of me? Not any more?

RUTH: I'm not scared of you.

WALLY: I don't know what happened. I want to apologize.

RUTH: No need.

WALLY: I had the feeling you were, somehow, putting me on.

RUTH: Why would I do that?

WALLY: Making fun . . .

RUTH: If anyone should apologize . . .

WALLY: You thought I was going to hurt you?

RUTH: I'll come across.

WALLY: What?

RUTH: I'll put out.

WALLY: It isn't that.

RUTH: Yes, it is.

WALLY: No!

RUTH *puts her hand on* WALLY'*s waist and slides it down over his buttocks, and on to his thigh.*

RUTH: I'll see you have a good time. Don't worry.

WALLY: Christ!

RUTH: I won't change my mind.

JOANNE *opens the door and walks into the living room.*

JOANNE: Hey, hey, hey!

WALLY *responds automatically to someone walking into the room at a moment of intimate contact and steps away from* RUTH.

JOANNE: I need a cigarette.

WALLY: I don't smoke.

JOANNE: What have you been doing?

RUTH: Not much. Talking. I don't have to ask . . .

JOANNE: You don't have to ask.

RUTH: Where's Mike?

JOANNE: Mike! Get your ass out of there!

RUTH: How was it?

JOANNE: On a scale of ten, I'd have to say, well, maybe seven. He had it there to make an eight, nine! He couldn't wait.

RUTH: You made it sound better than a seven.

JOANNE: I always try to kid myself I'm having a great time. What was going on in here? Did you two have a fight?

RUTH: You got Wally over-excited, with your carrying on.

MIKE *walks into the living room.*

WALLY: Hey!

MIKE: How you doing?

WALLY: Hanging-in.

JOANNE: Shit! Who wants to run out and get me a pack of cigarettes?

MIKE: Why don't you give up smoking?

WALLY: Looking good.

MIKE: All systems go.

JOANNE: The count-down got to three and then, the rocket launched prematurely.

MIKE: What are you talking!

JOANNE: Kidding. Just kidding. You were great.

MIKE: Better believe it.

WALLY: I gave up smoking six months ago.

MIKE: More than a year since I had a cigarette.

JOANNE: Applause, applause, applause! Bunch of fucking boy scouts. *(Searches for a pack of cigarettes)*

WALLY: What's the story?

MIKE: Tell you later.

The two men gravitate towards each other, isolating themselves from the two women.

WALLY: Pretty good?

WALLY: Pretty damn' good!

WALLY: Like the guys told you?

MIKE: Better.

WALLY: Jesus!

JOANNE *walks into the bedroom.*

MIKE: Ruthie, you want to fix me a drink?

RUTH: Sure. Why not? *(Walks into the kitchen)*

WALLY: She knows what it's all about?

MIKE: Now, she knows!

WALLY: You really gave it to her?

MIKE: Couldn't you hear?

WALLY: Like she was going into orbit! Christ!

MIKE: What can I tell you?

MIKE *and* WALLY *slap each other's hands, like two footballers, at the conclusion of a successfull play.*

WALLY: You mother!

JOANNE *walks into the living room.*

JOANNE: Who's going to make the bed? Ruthie?

RUTH *walks out of the kitchen.*

JOANNE: You want the sheets changed?

RUTH: I don't. Wally?

WALLY: What? Oh. No, look, it doesn't matter.

JOANNE: Right. Mike. Come and help me with the bed.

MIKE: Son-of-a-bitch!

MIKE *starts to laugh, as he walks into the bedroom.*

RUTH: Does Mike give Joanne a good report?

WALLY: Better than average.

RUTH: She's a difficult act to follow.

WALLY: You are sure . . .

RUTH: What?

WALLY: If you don't want to . . .

RUTH: What's making you so nervous?

WALLY: I don't know what we're doing.

RUTH: I'm not expecting any great experience.

WALLY: If you don't like me . . .

RUTH: I like you.

WALLY: . . . love . . .

RUTH: There's always an outside chance.

WALLY: It won't be the same . . .

RUTH: You might have hidden talents.

WALLY: I'm not like Mike.

RUTH: How do you know? Have you fucked Mike?

WALLY: What!

RUTH: How can you know what he's like in bed, if you haven't fucked him? You can't believe everything he says. You shouldn't believe anything! The last person . . .

MIKE *walks into the room.*

MIKE: There you go!

RUTH *offers* MIKE *a glass of scotch.*

MIKE: If he gives you any trouble, Ruthie, send for me.

RUTH: We'll make out.

MIKE: Save some of it for later.

RUTH: Don't you wish!

MIKE: Damn! You know what? You're making me feel horny.

RUTH: You want to throw a fuck into me.

MIKE: Wally, you're not up to this.

RUTH: Neither are you.

RUTH *puts a hand between* MIKE's *legs and* MIKE *steps away, quickly.*

JOANNE *walks into the living room.*

JOANNE: Like Confucius say, if merchant can't deliver, he shouldn't take order.

RUTH: You're fucking A-1 told!

RUTH *walks into the bedroom.*

MIKE: What are you waiting for?

WALLY *looks apologetically at* JOANNE, *and she laughs.*

MIKE: You don't want her to start without you.

WALLY *walks into the bedrom.*

JOANNE: Shut the door. It looks like Wally needs his privacy.

MIKE *closes the door.*

MIKE: You didn't have to get up right away.

JOANNE: Nothing better to do.

MIKE: What do you say? Why don't I stay on and keep you company, after Wally takes Ruth home?

JOANNE: No.

MIKE: I'm not in any hurry. I can stay the night.

JOANNE: Oh, shit!

MIKE: We could have breakfast.

JOANNE: You're not going to fall in love with me?

MIKE: What are you talking!

JOANNE: Don't make any big deal . . .

MIKE: Let's get to know each other?

JOANNE: I don't want to know you.

MIKE: Give it a chance, Joanne.

JOANNE: You're jerking off.

MIKE: We're going to see each other.

JOANNE: No, we're not.

MIKE: Come on! You can't kid me. You want some more.

JOANNE: No, I don't. It's different guys, Mike, every time I fuck. Nothing personal. I don't have relationships with the guys I screw. It gives them an unfair advantage. It's tough enough with strangers, if you dig it. Once let some guy get into you and start with his demands on time and effort, energy and obligation, you never get your head free, let alone your cunt.

MIKE: What demands? I'm not going to make demands. It's not going to be that kind of thing. No way! But you got to say, we make it . . . right? In bed, it's something special.

JOANNE: Whatever you say, champ.

MIKE: I can tell you . . .

JOANNE: You don't have to tell me. I was there. (Laughs)

MIKE: Why are you laughing?

JOANNE: Ruth really told you. What did you say to her?

MIKE: Right.

JOANNE: What did you say?

MIKE: I told her she was making me feel horny.

JOANNE: You do have yourself a way with people. I've got to say that. Especially women.

MIKE: Don't you know!

JOANNE: She grabbed you.

MIKE: Damn right! I thought she was going to take it out.

JOANNE: Just checking.

MIKE: What . . . checking?

JOANNE: Something you guys say. "Feeling horny." And "Getting a hard-on." "Ready when you are!" All that shit. Ruth was checking you out. Mostly, it's talk more than anything.

MIKE: You want to bet?

JOANNE: She had you jumping like she stuck a red-hot poker up your ass.

MIKE: What am I supposed to do? I'm supposed to let her grab me?   ·

JOANNE: Scared she might break it off?

MIKE: She was looking crazy.

JOANNE: Next time you're on the subway, grabbing yourself a piece of ass.

MIKE: What are you talking?

JOANNE: At a party . . .

MIKE: I don't grab ass!

JOANNE: What are you? A tit man? When you're grabbing a little girl's boobies, at the office . . .

MIKE: What makes you think . . .

JOANNE: Watch out! That's all. I'm telling you. We plan to start grabbing back.

MIKE: Any time, Jo. Be my guest!

JOANNE: Shit!

MIKE: Why do you have to . . .

JOANNE: It's got to hurt you more than us.

MIKE: The kind of language . . .

JOANNE: Don't you like your women talking dirty?

MIKE: It's pretty damn' unattractive.

JOANNE: Like getting drunk in public?

MIKE: Worse!

JOANNE: Something else we should keep for the proper time. When we're fucking? Oops! Making love. It seems to me you really get off . . .

MIKE: You don't have to talk dirty, if you want to get me off!

JOANNE: That's a pretty sentiment. What have I got to do? Kiss your ass?

MIKE: I can't talk to you!

JOANNE: You're going to tell me how to speak?

MIKE: I want you to know how people react.

JOANNE: You've been asking around?

MIKE: At the office.

JOANNE: I don't believe it!

MIKE: If you knew what they say . . .

JOANNE: Don't tell me.

MIKE: I guess the reason you don't have more responsibility . . .

JOANNE: I'm a woman.

MIKE: They don't discriminate.

JOANNE: The hell, they don't!

MIKE: The Fashion Editor's a woman.

JOANNE: No shit! What about the Sports Editor?

MIKE: Be reasonable. You don't expect . . .

JOANNE: Art Director?

MIKE: Barrett's assistant is a woman.

JOANNE: Is she any good?

MIKE: The best there is.

JOANNE: The best woman. If she's so fucking good, why isn't she Art Director? Will she be promoted, given Barrett drops dead?

MIKE: There's no reason why not.

JOANNE: If she promises she won't talk dirty around the office? As a rule, I only screw the help at their place. That way, I can get out quick, and I don't have this conversation. Shit! I don't want to talk about the office. Don't you get enough of that, all day?

MIKE: 'Kay. Okay. You got it. Come and sit here?

JOANNE: No.

MIKE: What's happening? Ruthie doesn't get off the way you do. You wouldn't know there was anybody in the bedroom. Maybe Wally needs help. What do you think?

JOANNE: I think he's getting all the help he can handle. How long have you been divorced?

MIKE: Two, three years.

JOANNE: You don't know exactly?

MIKE: Two years and seven months. Almost to the day.

JOANNE: How you doing?

MIKE: Pretty good. I never did like home-cooking.

JOANNE: Do you make the singles' bar circuit?

MIKE: Not really. I don't have to.

JOANNE: Falling over themselves?

MIKE: I wouldn't say that.

JOANNE: No.

MIKE: A guy, my age, and single. That's a novelty these days.

JOANNE: Suspect, too. You get your share of propositions from both sides of the fence, I should think.

MIKE: You got to be kidding.

JOANNE: No making a mistake?

MIKE: Nobody ever has.

JOANNE: Palling around with Wally, people don't get the idea . . .

MIKE: I don't! Christ! I hardly know the guy. I don't 'pal around' with him! What is that!

JOANNE: You never made it with another guy?

MIKE: What are you talking?

JOANNE: You never wanted to?

MIKE: Are you crazy?

JOANNE: Why did you get divorced?

MIKE: What does my getting divorced have to do . . . it doesn't have anything to do with . . . where do you get the idea?

JOANNE: I believe you.

MIKE: What kind of thing . . .

JOANNE: Why did you leave your wife?

MIKE: We got married out of college. We were both too young.

JOANNE: Ah.

MIKE: I was her first . . .

JOANNE: How long did you stay married to her?

MIKE: We lived together more than fifteen years. We had a trial separation for a time.

JOANNE: How long before you started cheating?

MIKE: I was faithful . . .

JOANNE: How long?

MIKE: The first couple of years I never so much as looked at another woman.

JOANNE: Two years.

MIKE: She got pregnant.

JOANNE: That was careless of her.

MIKE: Once she had the children . . .

JOANNE: You read that somewhere. Did she ever cheat on you?

MIKE: No.

JOANNE: If she did, you don't know.

MIKE: Emily was never unfaithful.

JOANNE: Shit! Don't go romantic on me! If she had the chance, you can bet she was giving it to everybody in the neighborhood. She's allowed. You were screwing around at the office. You can't expect she'll keep her legs crossed indefinitely. Why did you marry her right out of college? Did you have to?

MIKE: No.

JOANNE: She was your first real piece of ass. She had you pussy-whipped, and you weren't smart enough to know, if you can have one of us, you can have another, and if you can have another, you might as well! Still, you got your own back. You gave her the shaft. The poor, dumb cunt! What's she doing now? Has she gotten married again?

MIKE: No, she hasn't.

JOANNE: She's not waiting for you to come back?

MIKE: It's none of your damned business!

JOANNE: Are you going back?

MIKE: Emily is, in many ways, a remarkable woman. We were very much in love, when we got married, and for some time after, we were happy . . .

JOANNE: Why did you leave her?

MIKE: People change, as they get older.

JOANNE: Oh, shit! Why didn't I say that?

MIKE: Things we could share, when we were twenty . . .

JOANNE: You've got the whole thing off pat.

MIKE: . . . didn't seem equally important, fifteen years later.

JOANNE: Who's your analyst? I might give him a whirl.

MIKE: We both tried hard to keep the relationship alive.

JOANNE: The truth is, she couldn't fuck worth shit!

MIKE: For Christ's sake!

JOANNE: The tricks she did know couldn't get you off any more.

MIKE: You can't downgrade all human emotion . . .

JOANNE: Why not teach her some of the new tricks you were getting into?

MIKE: You can't simply reduce love to the level of appetite.

JOANNE: As far as I can get with love, I don't see what it has to do with fucking, which is one more body-contact sport, without sufficient superstars to make the game worth playing, on a regular basis.

MIKE: As much as you debase your own capacity for feeling, don't assume other people can't achieve meaningful associations.

JOANNE: Occasionally, I'd have to say, one time, maybe, in a hundred times at bat, it does give up a confrontation between two dedicated fanatics, which makes you want to hang in and wait for one more opportunity to blow your mind out.

MIKE: Tell Wally I'll call him later in the week.

JOANNE: Where are you going?

MIKE: What the hell! I'm going home.

JOANNE: Why?

MIKE: You must be kidding.

JOANNE: What's the rush?

MIKE: You've been trying to get rid of me . . .

JOANNE: No.

MIKE: I don't know what happened . . .

JOANNE: I said, you couldn't stay the night.

MIKE: After we got out of bed . . .

JOANNE: I don't want you telling yourself this is something more than it is.

MIKE: Your average one-night-stand?

JOANNE: Don't put yourself down.

MIKE: I guess I didn't make much of an impression.

JOANNE: You want to take another shot?

MIKE: Are you serious?

JOANNE: Sure. Why not?

MIKE: After Wally takes Ruth home?

JOANNE: All four of us. Together.

MIKE: Shit!

JOANNE: It's a king-size bed.

MIKE: Wally won't go for it.

JOANNE: How do you know?

MIKE: What about Ruth? Will she?

JOANNE: Ask her.

MIKE: Jesus!

JOANNE: Turns you on?

MIKE: You know it!

JOANNE: I thought it might.

MIKE: Did you have this all set up? From the beginning, did you figure we'd end up in bed together? All of us!

JOANNE: Group sex seemed to me the sort of thing you might enjoy.

MIKE: We're going to have a problem, persuading Wally.

JOANNE: Wally's not a swinger?

MIKE: If you knew the trouble I had, getting him here tonight.

JOANNE: He's keeping Ruthie occupied.

MIKE: I'm not saying he's a faggot.

JOANNE: He prefers to keep things one on one?

MIKE: He's a bit square. It scares him.

JOANNE: I'm hip.

MIKE: Suppose he doesn't go for it?

JOANNE: What?

MIKE: We don't need him.

JOANNE: Just you, and the two of us?

MIKE: Right!

JOANNE: Whatever.

MIKE: Christ!

JOANNE: We don't have to tell Wally. If you don't want to, we'll just let him go.

MIKE: How can we tell Ruth not to go home with him?

JOANNE: Ruth isn't going home tonight.

MIKE: 'Kay. Okay!

JOANNE: We won't tell him.

MIKE: I guess it's better if we don't.

JOANNE: Ever had two women at the same time, Mike?

MIKE: What are you talking!

JOANNE: Something your ex-wife would appreciate? Did you ever think . . .

MIKE: You bitch!

JOANNE: Might be just the thing . . .

MIKE: You've been putting me on!

JOANNE: You, and Emily, and Emily's best friend?

MIKE: You cunt!

JOANNE: I've had you, champ. I don't need a second go-round. It's too boring. Making out with the same guy twice. Unless he's really something special. You're not even average for a selfish prick.

MIKE *lashes out at* JOANNE. *He hardly makes contact, but the violence of the action throws him forward and he falls against her.*

JOANNE *steps back, casually.*

JOANNE: You want to use me, like a piece of meat. You have to know, the feeling's mutual.

MIKE *turns his back on* JOANNE *and walks towards the hallway which leads to the front door of the apartment. He fumbles with the locks, opens the door and walks out of the apartment. He closes the door behind him, gently.*

JOANNE *knocks on the bedroom door.*

JOANNE: Your time's up!

JOANNE *begins to tidy the room. She fetches a tray from the kitchen and puts it on the table. She stacks dishes on the tray.*

The bedroom door opens and WALLY *walks into the living room. He hesitates for a moment, in the doorway.*

WALLY: Where's Mike?

JOANNE: He went home.

WALLY: You're kidding!

JOANNE: He'll call you later in the week, he said.

WALLY: Son-of-a-bitch!

JOANNE: Something you had to tell him?

WALLY: No.

JOANNE: *(Calling)* Ruth!

WALLY: She won't be a minute.

JOANNE: Finishing herself off?

WALLY: What?

JOANNE: How was it?

WALLY: Why did Mike go home?

JOANNE: He ran out of things to say. You want to help me?

JOANNE *gives* WALLY *the tray and he takes it into the kitchen.*

JOANNE: You can put it anywhere.

RUTH *walks into the living room.*

JOANNE: What's happening?

RUTH: Not a lot. Where's Mike?

JOANNE: He went home.

WALLY: Son-of-a-bitch!

WALLY *walks out of the kitchen.*

JOANNE: Wally wanted to bring him up to date.

WALLY: He could have waited for me.

JOANNE: We'll take care of you.

RUTH: Did you have a fight?

JOANNE: You were very quiet in the bedroom. I thought you might have gone to sleep.

RUTH: There wasn't anything to make a noise about.

JOANNE: Wally didn't come up to expectations?

RUTH: I'm not sure how much I expected.

WALLY: I don't know what game you're playing . . .

JOANNE: Whatever! He didn't measure up?

RUTH: You could say . . .

WALLY: Shut up!

JOANNE *laughs.*

WALLY: You don't have to tell her.

JOANNE: Yes, she does.

WALLY: I don't have to listen.

JOANNE: You can always run out. The same as Mike!

RUTH: You did have a fight.

JOANNE: He wanted both of us to fuck him. Get rid of Wally, and then, all three of us, go to bed!

RUTH: He's got some imagination!

JOANNE: It didn't seem like anything you'd want to do.

RUTH: I guess I can go one night without getting myself laid.

JOANNE: Oh, sure! But if I'd known old Wally wasn't going to come through, I wouldn't have been so eager to get rid of

Mike. He's not much to write home about, still and all, he can deliver.

WALLY: Bitch! You bitch!

RUTH: That's more energy than I've seen out of him all night.

JOANNE: You guys! You're all the same. If you can't get off, you have to beat up on someone.

RUTH: Why don't the three of us jump into bed?

WALLY: I wouldn't! Shit! What do you think!

JOANNE: He's a faggot. Most likely he fucks Mike, nights they can't find themselves a piece of ass.

WALLY: You lying bitch!

JOANNE: Mike as good as told me.

WALLY: Mike sucks! If Mike said that . . .

RUTH: He's not a faggot. He just can't get it up.

WALLY: I can get it up. Don't you worry!

RUTH: Don't you wish!

WALLY: Any time!

RUTH: Just tonight you couldn't?

WALLY: Nobody . . .

JOANNE: Mike did all right.

WALLY: He's an animal. Mike would fuck a pig, if he couldn't buy a woman. He'd fuck a snake.

JOANNE: What does that make me!

WALLY: Another dumb cunt.

JOANNE: That's telling it, Wally, like it really is. Can you dig it, Ruth?

RUTH: Another dumb cunt.

WALLY: As long as you get down on your back and spread your legs, nobody gives a shit what you are!

JOANNE: He can make it now. He's got a hard-on now. Look at him! He'll fuck your ass!

WALLY: You know it!

JOANNE: Hey, champ! You're beautiful, when you're angry.

WALLY: You smart-ass, cock-sucking bitch!

JOANNE: Oh, baby! Sock it to me!

WALLY: I wouldn't let you kiss my ass!

RUTH: That's telling it!

JOANNE: That's the way it is.

WALLY: Believe it!

Silence.

JOANNE: You can go home now.

WALLY: I'll go when I'm good and ready.

JOANNE: Go now.

WALLY: You don't tell me what to do.

RUTH: You're fighting for your life.

WALLY: What are you talking?

JOANNE: Let up on us, we'll break your balls.

RUTH: Get out, Wally, while you can.

WALLY: You two! You make me laugh!

RUTH: How many children have you got? You told me. I forget.

WALLY: What?

RUTH: Do they look at all like you?

WALLY: What the hell!

RUTH: I don't see how you could get a rabbit pregnant, with that pea-shooter thing of yours. Always assuming you could get it up.

JOANNE: How does your loving wife get off?

RUTH: What would you do?

JOANNE: I don't favor mechanical substitutes.

RUTH: In the circumstances . . .

JOANNE: Oh, yes. But are those vibrators safe?

RUTH: In the right hands.

JOANNE: I hate anything to do with electricity.

RUTH: Do you have one of those? What are they called?

JOANNE: Dildo.

RUTH: Strap it on, and you can go all night.

JOANNE: How big do they make them?

RUTH: Can you get them in different colors?

JOANNE: What size does your wife prefer?

RUTH: What's it like, I wonder. Having a plastic prick stuck up your ass?

JOANNE: Better than nothing, I suppose.

RUTH: And nothing just about describes's Wally's sexual equipment. Hey! Why don't you show Joanne? She won't believe it, if she doesn't see it. Steve wasn't hung, but Wally makes him look like "The Amazing Colossal Man!" Did you see that movie?

JOANNE: Yes. Can you imagine . . .

RUTH: Wally's more like "The Incredible Shrinking Violet."

The two women pursue WALLY *around the room. They try to grab him, lunging at his genitals.*

RUTH: You didn't mind showing it to me.

JOANNE: Don't be shy.

RUTH: You wanted me to see it.

JOANNE: Anything for a laugh.

RUTH: You wanted me to tell you . . .

JOANNE *catches hold of* WALLY, *by the arm, and holds him.* RUTH *steps close to* WALLY, *and both women reach for his genitals.*

WALLY *reacts, frantically, and he pulls himself free.* WALLY *covers his genitals, with both hands.*

JOANNE *laughs.*

JOANNE: I'll show you mine, if you'll show me yours.

WALLY *backs into the hallway.*

The two women watch WALLY, *as he opens the door and runs out of the apartment.*

JOANNE *walks into the hallway and closes the door. She turns the lock and walks back into the living room.*

JOANNE: Well?

RUTH *starts to laugh.*

JOANNE *walks towards* RUTH *and puts both hands on the other woman's shoulders. The two women hold each other in a loose embrace and laugh. There is a suggestion of hysteria in the quality of their laughter.*

JOANNE *rocks* RUTH, *gently, and the two women begin to dance. They face each other and improvise a dance, which seems to have vaguely Greek inspiration. They slap each other's hands, diagonally, right hand against right hand, and then, left hand against left, in time to a dance step they invent.*

The two women chant a wordless song of triumph.

JOANNE *and* RUTH *stop dancing. They hold on to each other, tightly, in a passionate embrace.*

Ruth *shrugs out of the embrace, abruptly, and steps away from* Joanne.

Joanne: Ruthie. Are you all right?

Joanne *offers to take one of* Ruth's *hands.*

Joanne: What is it?

Ruth *shrugs and shakes her head.*

Ruth: *(Murmuring)* . . . nothing . . . no . . .

Joanne: *(Laughing)* You don't expect me to believe that?

Ruth: . . . had the same look on his face . . .

Joanne: Wally?

Ruth: When you said he was a homosexual?

Joanne: Yes?

Ruth: Do you remember?

Joanne: I remember calling him a faggot. I wasn't being serious.

Ruth: You remember how he looked?

Joanne: Sort of. Not very clearly. I was having too much fun. I remember what he said.

Ruth: Wouldn't let you . . .

Joanne: . . . kiss my ass!

The obscenity is an intrusion in the changing atmosphere, and both women react to it, Joanne, *as she speaks, and* Ruth, *as she hears the word spoken.*

Silence.

Ruth: . . . the same look . . .

Joanne: The young guy?

RUTH: Yes.

JOANNE: The night you came here?

RUTH: I started to think.

JOANNE: Oh, baby! Don't . . .

RUTH: I betrayed him!

JOANNE: What . . . betray?

RUTH: I told you want happened.

JOANNE: You had to tell someone.

RUTH: He made me promise I wouldn't say anything.

JOANNE: He didn't want you talking to the police.

RUTH: I wouldn't tell you . . . and Mike . . .

JOANNE: You didn't tell Mike?

RUTH: The last thing Wally said to me . . .

JOANNE: Wally!

RUTH: In the bedroom . . .

JOANNE: Are you talking about Wally?

RUTH: He begged me . . .

JOANNE: Wally made you promise not to say anything?

RUTH: He was so ashamed.

JOANNE: Of course, you're going to tell me. Wally must have known that. You didn't say anything to Mike.

RUTH: I would have told Mike.

JOANNE: I don't believe that.

RUTH: I wanted to hurt Wally.

JOANNE: You haven't told me. Not in any detail.

RUTH: He blamed me.

JOANNE: I'm not asking you to tell me.

RUTH: He said, "It's your fault!"

JOANNE: I'm not sure how much I want to know.

RUTH: "If you don't want to," he said.

JOANNE: The whole damn thing was my idea.

RUTH: I wanted to. He couldn't!

JOANNE: None of this would have happened . . .

RUTH: It was so ugly! He tried to make love to me, and he couldn't, and he just went on. It was obscene! He wanted to push himself into me, and his thing . . . he couldn't make it hard. I did everything I could . . .

JOANNE: Ruthie! I don't want to hear about it.

RUTH: I thought the idea was to tell each other . . .

JOANNE: The idea was to use them, the same way they use us, and let them know!

RUTH: You don't want to talk about having sex with them?

JOANNE: You didn't . . . have sex . . .

RUTH: Depends what you mean.

JOANNE: Right! I don't want to talk about it.

RUTH: You're blaming me.

JOANNE: No, I'm not.

RUTH: You think I wanted him . . .

JOANNE: You didn't have to stay there.

RUTH: He was on top of me.

JOANNE: You could have pushed him off.

RUTH: I was trapped.

JOANNE: You could have gotten away.

RUTH: My fault!

JOANNE: Don't get yourself into a panic here!

RUTH: It was your idea.

JOANNE: The whole damn' thing!

RUTH: You wanted to invite them over . . .

JOANNE: He's the original hundred pound weakling! I can't believe, however hard he tried, if you wanted to get away from him, I can't see Wally stopping you. I'm sorry. I wasn't there. I don't know what happened, and I don't want to know, if it's so ugly, I'd much rather not. For a moment, I guess, I was blaming you, and I don't have the right. Now, what else can I do? Get down on my knees and beg for your forgiveness? Lie down on the floor and kiss your big toe? Run out and fetch a gallon of chocolate chip ice cream for your holiness?

RUTH: You're not very funny.

JOANNE: Did you hear the one about . . .

RUTH: I don't want to. If it's like the other dirty jokes you told this evening.

JOANNE: I don't think they wanted me to tell them dirty jokes.

RUTH: Old, dirty jokes! No, I don't think they did.

JOANNE: What do you mean? Old! You really know how to hurt a guy!

RUTH: I'm not sure they enjoyed anything very much, after they finished eating.

JOANNE: Hey! I'm ready for bed. I don't know about you.

RUTH: Aren't we going to tidy up in here?

JOANNE: I'm not. Why? Are you?

JOANNE *walks into the bedroom.*

The telephone is on the floor beside the bedroom door. RUTH *picks up the receiver and dials a number.*

RUTH: Maria? . . . Yes. Did the children go to bed? . . . That's good. And no fuss?

JOANNE *walks into the living room. She looks at* RUTH, *briefly, and walks into the bathroom.*

RUTH: Are there any messages for me? Did anyone 'phone? . . . I'll see you in the morning, Maria. Goodnight.

RUTH *puts down the receiver.*

JOANNE: I wish you didn't have to do that.

JOANNE *walks into the living room.*

RUTH: What?

JOANNE: It really hurts my feelings.

RUTH: What are you talking about?

JOANNE: You were calling Maria. Checking up on the children?

RUTH: I have to make sure they're all right.

JOANNE: I guess so.

RUTH: I don't see why it hurts your feelings.

JOANNE: It closes me out.

RUTH: It's not meant to.

JOANNE: Any time we quarrel, after we make love, you call Maria and you ask about the children.

RUTH: That simply isn't true.

JOANNE: It makes me feel a little bit insecure.

RUTH: I can't pretend they don't exist. You don't want me to do that?

JOANNE: Yes, I do. I know you can't. It isn't rational. I want you to pretend the children don't exist.

RUTH: I can't do that.

JOANNE: You want to go to bed.

RUTH: We always get into some kind of argument, just before we go to bed.

JOANNE: I'm sorry. *(Laughing)* Why am I always apologizing to you?

JOANNE *makes a hesitant gesture. She reaches out to touch* RUTH.

JOANNE: We can watch the movie, if you don't want to sleep.

RUTH: I want to sleep.

JOANNE *switches off the table lamp beside the bathroom door and the two women walk into the bedroom.*

As they step through the doorway, RUTH *takes hold of* JOANNE's *hand.*

Silence.

[END OF ACT TWO]

ACT THREE

Night.

The living room is almost dark. There is a table lamp standing on the floor, behind the sofa. The room is noticeably more tidy now than it used to be. Books have been arranged on the bookshelves, and magazines have been stacked in tidy piles, some of them, admittedly, on the floor, but they are pushed back into the corner of the room.

The living room seems to be empty.

RUTH opens the front door and walks into the apartment. She takes her key out of the lock and closes the door.

RUTH: Jo-Jo?

RUTH is dressed for an evening at the theater, and dinner afterwards, at some fashionable restaurant.

RUTH: Jo-Jo!

JOANNE pushes herself up on to her knees and looks at RUTH leaning on the back of the sofa.

JOANNE: Hi!

RUTH reacts, visibly startled by JOANNE's unexpected appearance.

RUTH: What are you doing?

JOANNE: Did I make you jump?

RUTH: Yes.

JOANNE: I didn't aim to.

RUTH: What's going on?

JOANNE: I've been stood up.

JOANNE *puts the table lamp on the table at the end of the sofa.*

JOANNE: Richard called. Something he has to do. Something, he said, important. Whatever! He can't make it.

JOANNE *is wearing a T-shirt and an old pair of jeans.*

RUTH: You're not dressed.

JOANNE: I'm not! Heavens!

RUTH: You know what I mean.

JOANNE: I'm not going with you.

RUTH: Of course you are.

JOANNE: No, I'm not.

RUTH: Why not?

JOANNE: I don't want to.

RUTH: You can't be serious!

JOANNE: Yes.

RUTH: I've asked Tod to meet us here.

JOANNE: I've been catting around too much just lately. I never get any work done.

RUTH: You're going to stay home and work?

JOANNE: I'm going to stay home and work.

RUTH: Why didn't you let me know? You could have baby-sat the children for me.

JOANNE: When did you start calling me Jo-Jo?

RUTH: Maria's got a date.

JOANNE: It's a kid's name.

RUTH: I promised her the night off, she says. I spent half the day finding someone.

JOANNE: I wish you wouldn't.

RUTH: What?

JOANNE: You're better off without me hanging around.

RUTH: When did Richard call?

JOANNE: Not long ago. Just before you got here. Before I started to get dressed.

RUTH: You can find someone else.

JOANNE: Go through my little black book? I don't think so.

RUTH: You want to see the show. You got the tickets.

JOANNE: I don't want to spend another night on the town, with your good friend, Tod. I don't find him nearly so irresistable as you obviously do.

RUTH: I don't believe this!

JOANNE: Why don't you wait for Tod downstairs?

RUTH: Thanks a lot!

JOANNE: Spare us both the unnecessary embarrassment of having to be polite. He doesn't enjoy it any more than I do.

RUTH: What's gotten into you?

JOANNE: It used to be I could choose who came into my home!

RUTH: You're being idiotic!

JOANNE: Yes, I am. I guess. I don't know. Whatever! I don't like Tod. I do know that. I don't want to spend time with him. I don't have to!

RUTH: What have you got against him?

JOANNE: Oh, shit! *(Shakes her head and gestures apologetically)* I'm sorry.

RUTH: All right, then. I won't go.

Joanne: Now, who's being idiotic?

Ruth: I thought you liked Tod.

Joanne: Once upon a time . . . *(Laughs)*

Ruth: You introduced us to each other.

Joanne: You had to say that!

Ruth: He's more your friend . . .

Joanne: Share and share alike!

Ruth: . . . than he is mine.

Joanne: More than a friend?

Ruth: Why did you let me go ahead and arrange the evening? You could have stopped me.

Joanne: I didn't know you'd invite Tod.

Ruth: I look such an ass! Putting him off like this. At the last minute.

Joanne: You look stunning. As a matter of fact.

Ruth: Why can't we go to the theater?

Joanne: I'd rather stay at home.

Ruth: And if I don't want to?

Joanne: You don't have to.

Ruth: Hey! You make it sound like you don't care what I do. Go to the theater. Go to hell!

Joanne: It isn't going to the theater.

Ruth: Tod?

Joanne: I care what you do.

Ruth: You don't want me seeing Tod?

Joanne: Do you see him? How often do you see him?

Ruth: I had lunch with him.

JOANNE: When?

RUTH: Last week. Wednesday.

JOANNE: Did you tell me?

RUTH: Probably not.

JOANNE: Why not?

RUTH: Why should I? It's not important.

JOANNE: That's why you didn't tell me?

RUTH: Tod seemed to think it might be a good idea, if I didn't talk to you about him.

JOANNE: That's why you didn't tell me.

RUTH: That's why.

JOANNE: What reason? Why shouldn't you talk to me?

RUTH: He didn't elaborate.

JOANNE: You didn't ask him to?

RUTH: How could I?

JOANNE: What's the difficulty?

RUTH: I don't talk to other people about us.

JOANNE: I do.

RUTH: Yes?

JOANNE: Sure. Why not?

RUTH: What do you say?

JOANNE: I tell them you're the greatest fuck I ever had! Is it likely? Would I talk about you? What do you think?

RUTH: I don't know. If you tell me . . .

JOANNE: Shit! When you come on, with that dumb cunt expression in your voice, I want to kick your ass!

RUTH *laughs*.

JOANNE: Will you get out of here?

RUTH: The delicacy of your sentiment is only surpassed by the elegance of your phrasing.

JOANNE: Right! Okay! Everybody knows you went to Barnard. You don't have to advertise.

RUTH: Did you finish grade school?

JOANNE: What grade school! In my neighborhood, anybody who went to school was automatically a sissy and got beaten up on their way home. Shit! Don't you know? Too much book-learning will drive you crazy. Didn't your Daddy tell you?

RUTH: I thought you went blind?

JOANNE: No, no. That's playing with yourself. Where did I put my glasses?

RUTH *laughs, in spite of herself, and* JOANNE *grins at her.*

JOANNE: Do I have to get dressed up and traipse around all night? I don't want to. Tell the truth, the very last goddamn thing!

RUTH: You don't have to.

JOANNE: Lady, you're a prince!

RUTH: We'll stay home.

JOANNE: If you were a guy, I'd kiss you.

RUTH: What are we going to say to Tod?

JOANNE: Whatever! You better say it. I'll tell the ass-hole to go fuck himself.

RUTH: I thought you were going to do something about that?

JOANNE: I quit smoking. Do I have to stop talking dirty? Shit! What do you leave a guy?

RUTH: What is this stuff? What have you been doing? *(Looks at the photographs and rough copy spread out on the floor)*

JOANNE: Don't laugh. I've been working.

RUTH: What's the story?

JOANNE: If I tell you the story, you won't buy the magazine.

RUTH: I won't buy it anyway.

JOANNE: Oh, thanks!

RUTH: I don't buy magazines.

JOANNE: Am I being a pain? I don't want to ruin your evening.
If it's just the theater. I can make the theater.

The house telephone buzzes.

JOANNE: You want to get that?

RUTH *picks up the receiver of the house telephone.*

RUTH: Tod? . . . Hi, there . . . Yes, it's Ruth. Why don't you
come on up? . . . I know. Yes, I know it's getting late!

JOANNE *presses the switch, beside the house telephone, which opens
the front door to the apartment building, automatically.*

JOANNE: He can't come up, if you don't let him in?

RUTH: Have you got the door? Tod? *(Hangs up the receiver of
the house telepone)* I guess he's on his way.

JOANNE: I guess.

RUTH: He was asking, what are we doing?

JOANNE: Why does he make you so nervous?

RUTH: Don't we know it's getting late. I'm not nervous.

JOANNE: You're acting like a scholgirl.

RUTH: I am not!

JOANNE: Take my word.

RUTH: Are you going to get changed?

JOANNE: You're blushing.

RUTH: You can't go to the theater dressed like that.

JOANNE: Have you gone to bed with him?

RUTH: Tod's going to be here . . .

The house telephone buzzes and JOANNE *picks up the receiver.*

JOANNE: Yes? . . . Right. *(Presses the switch, which opens the front door, and hangs up the receiver)* He sent the taxi away. Something in your voice?

RUTH: I promised him . . .

JOANNE: You told me. I know. Have the two of you made love?

RUTH: Yes.

JOANNE: Before you had lunch? Afterwards? You don't have to tell me, if you don't want to.

RUTH: I don't have to tell you anything.

JOANNE: You have the right to remain silent.

RUTH: One thing. More than anything!

JOANNE: The way I make a joke?

RUTH: You know it!

JOANNE: Drives you bananas?

RUTH: Hiding the pain!

JOANNE: Laugh, Pagliacci!

RUTH: Shit!

JOANNE: *(Laughs)* Tod won't like that, Ruthie. Ladies aren't supposed to use bad language.

RUTH: You don't want to hide the pain. What pain there is. Much less than meets the eye.

JOANNE: Hey!

RUTH: You want us all to know, suffering! I'm suffering! Pity me!

JOANNE: You bitch!

RUTH: Oh, yes. Now! That's more like it.

JOANNE: Turns you on, when I call you names? I didn't know.

RUTH: The first . . . tonight . . . the only true thing . . .

The doorbell rings.

RUTH: Why is that?

JOANNE: Meet Connie Concern! Fuck you, lady!

RUTH *opens the front door.*

JOANNE: Hey, stud! How you doing? Come on in.

TOD *walks into the apartment and closes the door.*

TOD: You do know what time it is?

JOANNE: It must be getting late.

TOD: Yes, if we want to make the theater.

JOANNE: Ruthie's here. All trembling, with breathless anticipation.

RUTH: We're not going to the theater.

TOD: Okay. Fine. I hear it's terrible, anyway. Why don't we just have dinner? Where's your date?

JOANNE: You two run along. I'm on a diet. Well, it's more like I'm starving myself to death. Seems appropriate, don't you think?

TOD: Ruth?

RUTH: Let's have a drink.

TOD: What have you got?

JOANNE: What do you want?

TOD: Scotch?

RUTH: Coming up.

RUTH *walks into the kitchen.*

TOD: Have you two been quarrelling?

JOANNE: Why, Toddy! What makes you think? You are the ass-hole of the world! Do you know that? Shit! What can Ruthie see in a prick like you?

TOD: Maybe you should ask her.

JOANNE: You were going to call Ruthie and arrange to meet her at the theater.

TOD: I didn't have time. I'm sorry. I didn't realize it was important.

JOANNE: You didn't realize! You don't give a shit!

RUTH *carries two glasses into the living room. She gives one of them to* TOD.

TOD: Thanks.

RUTH: You don't have to whisper. I can still hear you.

JOANNE: I'm surprised your ears weren't burning most of the afternoon. Toddy and I had lunch today. That's a novelty right there. We went Dutch. Naturally! I wouldn't have it any other way. Well, I might consider going French, with some other guy, you understand, and in another situation. The waiters at La Scala get upset if the customers start going down on one another. *(Shakes her head and grins, ruefully)* I'm doing it again.

RUTH: You had lunch with Tod?

JOANNE: You don't seem particularly surprised.

RUTH: Why should I be surprised? You're old friends. Old friends do have lunch.

JOANNE: Are you at all surprised?

RUTH: If you're asking, did I know?

JOANNE: Did you know?

RUTH: No, I didn't.

JOANNE: It wasn't your idea?

TOD: I told you, Jo-Jo . . .

JOANNE: I have the strongest disinclination to believe you, Toddy. Whatever you say!

TOD: Ruth didn't know we were having lunch.

JOANNE: Right! You used to call me Jo-Jo! I remember. Shit! I used to hate that.

RUTH: You had lunch with Tod, and you talked about me?

JOANNE: Among other things. Yes, I'd have to say, the main thrust of our conversation, Toddy, wouldn't you agree?

TOD: I'm sorry, Ruth. I should have told you.

RUTH: I think so.

JOANNE: It seems we kept our secret better than we thought possible. Toddy came to me, asking advice on the best way to persuade you into marrying him. Can you dig it?

RUTH: Tod knows about us. I told him. Tod, I told you, the first time we went to bed.

JOANNE: Oh, shit!

RUTH: You didn't tell him? What? Like, we're just "good friends!" I don't believe it!

JOANNE: What did you tell him?

RUTH: We're lovers.

JOANNE: What was that routine at lunch?

TOD: If you didn't want to tell me . . .

RUTH: Why didn't you tell him?

JOANNE: How many other people have you told?

RUTH: Nobody else.

JOANNE: You haven't told your children?

RUTH: Nobody else cared enough to ask.

TOD: You're not ashamed?

JOANNE: No. Goddamn it!

TOD: Something precious? You don't want to share?

RUTH: Why pretend you didn't know?

TOD: If Jo-Jo had been forthcoming, I would have told her. She wanted to play games. I was happy to accomodate her.

JOANNE: That was some number you did on me.

TOD: You told me everything I wanted to know.

JOANNE: I told you shit!

TOD: What you didn't say . . .

RUTH: Did you tell her we'd been to bed?

TOD: Certainly.

RUTH: And you pretended? Why?

JOANNE: I didn't believe him. I had to ask you.

TOD: Checking up on me? I always tell the truth, Jo-Jo. I may not tell the whole truth.

JOANNE: You said you didn't talk to people about us. Shit! And I believed you!

RUTH: You didn't tell me it was meant to be a secret.

TOD: Ruth didn't talk to people.

JOANNE: She told you!

TOD: Yes. And talking about you . . .

JOANNE: I don't want to hear!

TOD: . . . she was very loving. It seemed to me, you might represent a threat.

JOANNE: Right!

RUTH: I was frightened.

JOANNE: We can't lie to each other.

RUTH: You were angry.

JOANNE: Frightened?

RUTH: Something to do with Tod, and if I told you . . .

TOD: Were you guys talking about me?

RUTH: I couldn't tell you.

TOD: I'm flattered.

JOANNE: You fucking comedian!

TOD *laughs.*

JOANNE: You want a good trick? Why don't you bend over, Toddy, and shove your head right up your ass?

TOD: I have to tell you, Jo-Jo. It wasn't much of a surprise, when Ruthie told me. I always had my suspicions. When we were having our own 'brief encounter' . . .

JOANNE: Shit!

TOD: If there is one area in which Ruth is critical . . .

JOANNE: Now might be a good time for you to leave.

TOD: In point of fact, neither one of you told the other.

JOANNE: I told Ruth we had lunch.

TOD: Under pressure.

RUTH: I told Joanne we went to bed.

TOD: You didn't run straight back to her and say, "Tod and I made love."

RUTH: No.

TOD: Jo-Jo didn't call you this afternoon and say, "Tod took me out to lunch." Did she tell you we had an affair?

JOANNE: Oh, please! Don't exaggerate!

TOD: We went to bed.

JOANNE: I told her.

RUTH: You didn't tell me.

JOANNE: I said we were old friends. I left you to draw your own conclusions.

TOD: You didn't spell it out? So there could be no making a mistake?

RUTH: Why didn't you tell me?

JOANNE: I tell you too much. I'm not sure how well you cope. I don't want you to think I might have slept with the entire male population of New York City!

TOD: And many of the more attractive women.

JOANNE: *(Laughing)* Even if it's true.

TOD: Your modesty does you credit.

JOANNE: What happened to your wife, Tod? Did she try to kill herself? I don't remember. Did she leave you? Was that the story? You told me something . . .

TOD: She didn't kill herself.

JOANNE: Did she try?

TOD: I've told Ruthie all about Elaine.

JOANNE: And then she left you?

TOD: She left me.

JOANNE: Why was that?

TOD: You want to tell Ruth about the man who cut his wrists?

JOANNE: Why don't you? I've told the story so many times, it's really boring. Anyway, he didn't die.

TOD: Does she know about the woman who left her husband?

JOANNE: Oh, Christ! Not that fairy story!

TOD: Have you told her?

JOANNE: She went back to her loving husband, and they had another kid. As if there aren't enough kids in the world! It was a very therapeutic experience all around.

TOD: Did she tell you . . .

JOANNE: Anything remotely interesting, I told Ruth. Anything I thought might get a laugh. I didn't tell her shit about you.

TOD: Why did you introduce us?

JOANNE: She thinks the only selfish prick in the world is her ex-husband.

TOD: Steve?

JOANNE: I wanted to show her . . .

TOD: He's not such a bad guy.

JOANNE: Compared to you?

TOD: She could have done worse.

JOANNE: For example?

TOD: Ruth doesn't appreciate the way you always put him down. It makes her feel stupid.

JOANNE: Marrying Steve was pretty stupid!

TOD: You want some advice . . .

JOANNE: Not from you. Thanks all the same.

TOD: In your own best interests . . .

JOANNE: Shit!

TOD: Don't try so hard to make the rest of us look bad. It doesn't make you look better.

JOANNE: If you've got my best interests at heart, the Pope's a front man for the JDL.

TOD: I guess you must have a certain novelty value for Ruth.

JOANNE: I used to make you laugh.

TOD: When that wears off . . .

JOANNE: Don't hold your breath!

TOD: I figured, when you brought the two of us together . . .

JOANNE: Why did I do that!

TOD: . . . you were trying to unload her.

JOANNE *laughs.*

JOANNE: We're better suited, you and I.

TOD: I told you, at the time.

JOANNE: You said you were going to fuck me across ten states. I'm not sure we got over the first state line, before you started taking rain checks.

TOD: I found the reality wasn't anything like as stimulating as the fantasy I had.

JOANNE: You know it!

TOD: Making love to you, Joanne, is not unlike being run down by a truck.

JOANNE: You put me on like a fucking glove, and jerked yourself off!

RUTH *shouts wildly.*

The shouts are sounds, not words. They are angry sounds, desperate, without specific meaning. They seem to indicate a growing panic, which has overwhelmed RUTH's *capacity to articulate the sense of her outburst.*

Instinctively, JOANNE *reaches out to take hold of* RUTH, *to comfort her, and ease her pain.*

RUTH *pulls away from* JOANNE.

RUTH: Animals! Like animals! Not people. Making pain. Listen! Why must people? Can't you hear yourselves? Loving, why can't you be more, and not anger, all the time, hating! Fuck! Get the fuck out! What the fuck! Fuck off! Go fuck yourself! You dumb fuck! Shit! I'll fuck your ass!

The obscene violence seems to exhaust itself, and JOANNE *reaches a hand to* RUTH, *offering comfort.*

RUTH: Kisses, clumsy fingers, pushing in between my legs, pushing into me and his thing. He couldn't wait for me. He came, and I didn't feel anything. Some momentary pain, I can remember, and the humiliation, like what we did was somehow shameful, and we wouldn't ever talk about it, and we never did. He must have told his friends. They never treated me in quite the same way afterwards. He never talked to me again. I knew what he looked like, with his jeans pushed down around his ankles. I knew what happened to his thing, and I felt sorrow for him. I could feel his flesh inside my flesh. It was my first time, and I won't forget one minute of the ugly degradation, lying on my back, with my skirt bundled up around my waist, my panties torn and dragged to one side, and my legs, stuck up in the air, the sweating smell, the suffocating heat, inside that car, on that back seat, and if I look down far enough into my memory, I can find the marks the leather buttons made on my buttocks. Eighteen, I guess, going on twenty.

JOANNE: Ruth . . . baby . . .

RUTH: What love? Where?

TOD: Let me take you home.

TOD *offers a hand, tentatively.*

RUTH *stares at him, blankly, past him, and into her agony.*

RUTH: Face it, Ruth! You're not the most exciting fuck I ever had! Don't want to hurt your feelings. Just the same, you have to know, if I went looking out for someone else, it wasn't my fault altogether.

TOD: Jesus Christ!

RUTH: I'm going to come! Come with me! Come! Oh, baby! *(A paroxysm of rage shakes her and she shouts, wildly)* Can't! I can't! I never have! How can I? There's no caring. Nothing . . . love . . . *(Looks directly into* JOANNE'*s face and whispers her most painful, dark and secret discovery)* A piece of ass! Shit! A piece of meat! Know what I'm saying? Hey, lady! Pretty nice tits! Got time for a quickie? We can go to your place. You'll have a good time, I guarantee. What's your hurry? What are you running off? Cunt! Dumb-ass broad! Cock-sucker! On your belly, whore! Suck! And easy with the teeth!

Silence.

TOD: She can't stay here.

JOANNE: Get out of here, Tod.

Their mutual concern for RUTH *moderates the violence of their antagonism for a time.*

TOD: You're making her crazy.

JOANNE: You want to run that by me a second time!

TOD: It's you talking. All that filth!

JOANNE: If that's the way you want to handle it.

TOD: What else?

RUTH: . . . sorry . . . I'm sorry . . .

JOANNE: It's all right.

TOD: Ruth, why don't I take you home?

JOANNE: She's staying here tonight.

TOD: Can't you see, Joanne? She doesn't want to.

RUTH: You must have thought, poor thing, she's demented.

JOANNE: For a moment there, I'd have to say . . .

RUTH: . . . don't remember . . . all I said . . .

JOANNE: I'll run it down for you, as soon as Tod gets out of here.

TOD: I won't fight you.

JOANNE: The best thing, in the circumstances . . .

TOD: I don't want to make things worse.

JOANNE: A dignified retreat?

TOD: You should get away.

JOANNE: A winter cruise?

TOD: Away from Joanne! The longer you stay here . . .

JOANNE: Tod was going to call you this afternoon, so we could avoid this confrontation.

TOD: Granted, I have a special interest . . .

JOANNE: You don't have to stay and hear this.

TOD: It only makes me more concerned.

JOANNE: Lie down, why don't you? Rest.

TOD: I hate to see you lose yourself.

JOANNE: If I was crabby, when you got home . . .

RUTH: You weren't.

JOANNE: Yes, I was. Acting up a storm! I thought you set the whole thing up, because you couldn't face telling me yourself. Sorry about that! I underestimated Toddy, which was really dumb of me.

RUTH: Tell you what?

JOANNE: I don't know. Whatever! Something about you and Tod. He made his intentions pretty clear at lunch. I thought you wanted him to break the news, and I was, well, I wasn't too happy.

TOD: What makes you think Ruth would do that? Send me along to tell you something she knows is bound to wipe you out. Is that the way you expect people to behave? Is that the way you let people treat you, as a general rule? Why do you let them? You must not think too much of yourself.

JOANNE: I think a great deal of myself. Make no mistake. In or out of bed, I am the greatest! I don't let anyone kick shit in my face. Strike that! In Ruth's case . . .

TOD: Would she, do you think?

JOANNE: Ask her, why don't you?

TOD: Ruth?

RUTH: . . . lied to you . . .

JOANNE: Oh, sure! Why not?

RUTH: I let you think I hadn't told anyone.

JOANNE: It's not important. Anyway, you don't have to tell them. People see us out together once or twice, they're going to talk. You can't stop them.

TOD: I didn't know. Until Ruth told me.

JOANNE: You don't know shit!

JOANNE *struggles to control the normal, uninhibited flow of her vocabulary. Each failure to do so causes her visible distress.*

TOD: If not for your own sake, Jo-Jo, can't you think of Ruth?

JOANNE: Toddy, you're so thoughtful, kind and considerate!

TOD: You might try to spare her. Obviously, she finds it offensive.

JOANNE: Your consideration sucks! I'm sorry, Ruth. If I'm going to fight the mother-fucker, I can't tie both hands behind my back, and cut my tongue out.

TOD *laughs.*

JOANNE: You're treating us like kids. You're playing with us. Trying to manipulate! You've got your game plan set and nothing we do can affect the outcome. You think! Suppose we change the rules?

TOD: You, maybe. Ruthie? I don't think so. The rules I play by suit her. I doubt she wants to change them. What does she have to gain?

JOANNE: Two reasons why you couldn't let me know Ruth told you about us. Number one, you didn't want to think about my feelings, when you declared your serious intention! Am I right? Asking Ruth to marry you. Christ! You gave me the shaft, and at the same time, number two! I didn't have a chance to get back at you, because, dumb cunt that I am! I assumed you couldn't know what was happening to me.

TOD: I didn't want to hurt you.

JOANNE: Blow it out your ass!

TOD: I was simply looking for the most effective way of eliminating you.

JOANNE: I'm hip.

TOD: Ruthie, you should tell Joanne.

Silence.

RUTH: We talked about it.

TOD: What did we talk about?

RUTH: The possibility . . .

TOD: More than that.

JOANNE: Whatever! You talked?

RUTH: Tod asked me to marry him.

TOD: You may not want to believe this, Jo-Jo. I want to cause you as little pain . . .

JOANNE: I don't believe it.

TOD: I'm very fond of you.

JOANNE: In a rat's ass!

TOD: I happen to think you're a bad influence . . .

JOANNE: What did you tell him?

TOD: I'll take Ruthie home.

JOANNE: What did you say?

TOD: She needs to rest.

JOANNE: If Ruth is dumb enough to pick up on your proposition, you want to tell me how you persuaded her she'd be so much better off with you?

TOD: I didn't have to twist her arm.

JOANNE: How did you sell her?

TOD: I don't imagine you want to hear about the more intangible, the intimate . . .

JOANNE: Love, honor and obey? No, I'll take that as read. You concentrate on the financial settlement. Is it drawn up on a pay or play basis? I mean, either way, does Ruth come out ahead? Or do you get it all back, when she leaves?

TOD: She won't leave.

JOANNE: Do you know what you've got there? She'd leave God, if he wasn't dynamite in bed. Toddy, you don't have the stamina. You're pretty good. Once a night, and on your own terms. She's had that. She left that when she came to me.

TOD: She was desperate.

JOANNE: Is that what she said?

TOD: The way you concentrate on the sexual aspects, only demonstrates how shallow your feelings are for Ruth, and I have to say, how tenuous the relationship . . .

JOANNE: We sleep together.

TOD: I know.

JOANNE: We make love.

TOD: Ruthie told me.

JOANNE: What did she tell you?

TOD: She doesn't have your gift for descriptive detail!

JOANNE: You must be glad of that.

TOD: She made it clear enough.

JOANNE: It doesn't shock you?

TOD: Yes.

JOANNE: You can live with it?

TOD: She's had a bad experience.

JOANNE: Why does Ruth want to sleep with other women?

TOD: She's been hurt.

JOANNE: A temporary aberration?

TOD: It's not a permanent condition.

JOANNE: You'll get her back . . .

TOD: In my opinion . . .

JOANNE: . . . on the straight and narrow?

TOD: . . . it has more to do with you.

JOANNE: That's neat!

TOD: She's become attached to you.

JOANNE: Once you get her away . . .

TOD: She's very susceptible.

JOANNE: I didn't force anything . . .

TOD: Easily influenced!

JOANNE: It's not like that. We don't have the necessary apparatus! If I wanted to rape her, I'd have to buy a prick. Rape is, essentially, a masculine activity. Men, women, dogs and sheep. The target doesn't seem to matter all that much. You've got to have a prick, and it's better with a hard-on, I suppose.

TOD: When she doesn't see you . . .

JOANNE: One thing, I must say . . .

TOD: Yes! When I get her away!

JOANNE: . . . I admire your determination. Given, you won't know if she's sleeping with the maid, any time you leave the house! You know what I'm saying? It's got nothing to do with me. For the moment, yes, she's in love with me.

TOD: I don't understand how she can spend time with you.

JOANNE: I think you are.

TOD: Much less, make love!

JOANNE: If you're ever going to speak, you couldn't choose a better time.

TOD: You may think I'm not facing up to this.

RUTH: I'm not a trophy! Up for grabs!

TOD: I won't acknowledge what you do, when you're in bed.

RUTH: Winner take all!

JOANNE: I bet you think we kiss a lot. Hold hands and cuddle.

TOD: When two people love each other, I can accept they want to sleep together.

JOANNE: Score one for you!

TOD: No matter how limited the experience may be. How inadequate the sexual response.

JOANNE: Better than nothing?

TOD: I don't understand how Ruth, and you! Not another woman. You! I know you! The last person . . .

JOANNE: You don't know me, Toddy. For the record! I don't mean to interrupt. Go on. This is fascinating!

TOD: Let me take you home?

JOANNE: Aren't you supposed to go down on your knees?

TOD *lunges at* JOANNE *and catches hold of her by the shoulders. He shakes her violently.*

TOD *makes sounds, as he assaults* JOANNE, *but they are more like the noises an animal makes, grunting and barking.* JOANNE *is petrified. She cannot begin to defend herself. Her body is jerked backwards and forwards, and her mouth gapes open, as she gasps for breath.*

RUTH *forces herself between* JOANNE *and* TOD. *She breaks* TOD'*s hold on* JOANNE *and pushes him away from her.* JOANNE *stumbles back and* RUTH *turns to follow her.* RUTH *takes hold of* JOANNE.

TOD *makes a threatening, throaty growl, as he lurches towards the two women. He pushes past* RUTH, *throwing her sideways, and out of his way, as he pursues* JOANNE *into the corner of the living room.*

JOANNE *covers her face with her arms as* TOD *lumbers towards her. She blocks the first of his clumsy blows and then,* TOD *takes hold of her arms, viciously. He pulls* JOANNE *forward and spins her around. He pitches her across the room.*

JOANNE *stumbles into the sofa and turns quickly to face* TOD.

TOD *hits* JOANNE *and* RUTH *screams.*

JOANNE *slumps down, falling on to the floor behind the sofa.* RUTH *throws herself headlong at* TOD *and hits him on the chest, with both hands.* TOD *defends himself awkwardly against the attack.*

RUTH: God damn you!

TOD *catches hold of* RUTH'*s wrists and grips them tightly. He prevents* RUTH *from hitting him, and drags her towards the sofa.* RUTH *lashes out with her foot, and kicks* TOD *on the shin.*

TOD: Son-of-a-bitch!

TOD *throws* RUTH *on to the sofa. He leans forward and hits her across the face.* RUTH *pulls back into the corner, and cowers away from* TOD, *abjectly.*

TOD *pulls* JOANNE *up on to her feet and tosses her on to the sofa, next to* RUTH. JOANNE *keeps herself at a safe arm's length, and watches* TOD, *anxiously.*

TOD: I ought to bang your heads together. What are you doing? Christ! You both want your asses kicking!

The two women watch TOD, *apprehensively.*

TOD: You don't like that? No. Well, that's what it's all about. Don't tell me we're equal. No way! Men and women! We're no more equal than the rabbit and the fucking snake! *(Laughs)* That's better. That's how I like it. No more arguments. Nothing to say. 'Cause you know what's going to happen, if you talk back. Christ! Why did I take all that? I should have done this right away. I should have let you see there's no percentage. Can you dig it! All that shit! Putting on a show for Ruthie. She's not impressed. Any more than I am. I know you, Joanne. You're scared. Shit scared! You never had a guy beat up on you before? With all your half-ass cracks, I would have bet you'd take more punches than a fighter with his arms cut off. You want to know the truth? The way things are, you still meet a guy, who won't hit a woman. Well, you're going to change all that. You want equality? There's all kinds, and some of them you won't like. Get smart with me, you have to know, there's a limit to the shit I'm going to take, and then, watch out! *(Hits the palm of his left hand with his right fist)* You want to fuck? We can fuck. The three of us. Together! Sounds good to me. I'm feeling horny.

TOD *takes hold of* JOANNE's *arm and drags her forward.* JOANNE *pulls away from* TOD, *leaning back against* RUTH.

TOD: I wouldn't fuck you, lady, if you were the last cunt in the western world. What do you think? After all the shit you laid on me, I'm going to climb in bed! I'd just as soon fuck a pig. *(Lets go of* JOANNE's *arm)*

JOANNE: Shouldn't you find out how the pig feels about that.

TOD *lunges forward and catches hold of* JOANNE. *He pulls her off the sofa and holds her in front of him, lifting her up on to her toes.*

TOD: You make me laugh. With all your talking, what are you? When you get to the nitty-gritty! When the chips are down, and it's put up, or shut up! What have you got to say? I can't hear you, Joanne. What have you got to say?

RUTH: Don't hurt her.

TOD: Am I hurting you? Shall I let go? You want me to let go?

RUTH: Let go of her.

TOD: Ask me nicely. I'll let go.

JOANNE: I won't ask shit from you.

TOD *covers* JOANNE's *mouth with one hand and he puts the other hand on her throat, in a spasm of almost homicidal rage.*

RUTH *jumps up and takes hold of* TOD's *arms. She hits at the hand, which is clasped around* JOANNEs *throat.*

TOD *relaxes his hold on* JOANNE *and steps back. He turns away.*

JOANNE *puts her hands up to her throat and massages it, gently.*

TOD: . . . sorry . . . I'm sorry . . . didn't mean . . .

JOANNE: 'Kay. Okay. No big deal.

TOD *turns and looks at* JOANNE.

TOD: I was trying to kill you.

JOANNE: I'm hip. You might talk to someone about those homicidal tendencies.

TOD: I'm serious.

JOANNE: Darling, so am I.

TOD *walks towards* JOANNE.

TOD: I would have killed you . . .

JOANNE *takes a quick step back.*

The two women put the sofa between TOD *and themselves.*

TOD: . . . if Ruthie hadn't tried to stop me.

JOANNE: Score one for Ruth.

TOD: I wanted to kill you.

JOANNE: It's all right. No harm done. Relax.

TOD *moves a hand towards his stomach. He hesitates, and then, turns his back on the two women.*

JOANNE: What's the matter, Ace?

TOD *walks into the bathroom and closes the door.*

RUTH: Are you all right?

JOANNE: I guess so. You want to get that maniac out of here?

RUTH: I was scared to death.

JOANNE: You were scared!

RUTH: What's he doing?

JOANNE: An educated guess? He's had some kind of accident and he's cleaning himself up.

RUTH: What accident?

JOANNE: Whatever! Our best chance of getting him out is not let him know we know.

RUTH: I don't know!

JOANNE: Use your imagination.

The bathroom door opens and TOD *walks into the living room.*

JOANNE: Everything okay?

TOD: Yes. It's fine. Thanks.

JOANNE: Great.

TOD: Ruthie, you want to go home?

RUTH: Oh, no.

TOD: I'll take you home. We can have dinner, if you like? It's not too late.

RUTH: I don't think so. Not tonight.

TOD: I'll get a taxi.

RUTH: No!

Silence.

TOD: I'd like to take you home.

RUTH: I'm not going home. Not yet.

TOD: You're staying here?

RUTH: Maybe. I don't know.

TOD: I want to marry you.

Silence.

TOD: I guess, if you want to stay here . . .

JOANNE: She wants to stay.

TOD: What will you do? Go right to bed? Hit the sack and stay there, till it's time to get back home? Who put the kids to bed? Who takes care of them? What will you do? Take the bitch to live with you? Tell the kids she's their aunt? That's a switch! When I was growing up, if your mother brought a fella home, he was your uncle . . . right? I never figured you for a dyke. You really get off, when the bitch goes down on you? Do you take turns? First one, and then the other? What is that? You were married for ten years. The way you tell it, Steve wasn't all that much in the bed department. I've got to say, any man, with half a prick, is better than a dyke, with her tongue, two hands, and all ten of her fingers!

JOANNE: Any time she gets lonesome for the real thing, I'll buy her a licorice stick, and she can suck on that.

TOD: It won't last. It can't last! The bitch will meet someone else she has to fuck. She's had you. She'll start looking round. You have to know that. You'll get tired of her cheap cracks and her dirty talk. You're not like her. She goes either way. Nothing means anything to her. She uses men, the same way she's using you. It's all for her own satisfaction. She doesn't give anything.

JOANNE: I didn't give anything to you.

TOD: Damn right!

JOANNE: I didn't get anything.

TOD: A lot of whores are dykes. Did you know that?

JOANNE: What does it tell you?

TOD: Women, who sell themselves, make out with strangers. They can't deal with a one-on-one, meaningful relationship.

JOANNE: Something you know about. You're always fucking strangers. The only friend you've got left is your prick, and it won't stand up for you much longer.

TOD: Right! I've got my prick!

JOANNE: And a pretty thing it is.

TOD: You know it!

RUTH: You want to take it out and show us?

JOANNE: Hey!

RUTH: We just can't hardly wait.

Something like the camaraderie, which united the two women in their assault on MIKE *and* WALLY, *reasserts itself.*

JOANNE: Oh, wow! Do we get to see it?

TOD: Could be the reason men aren't enough for you, you're not making it for them.

RUTH: Why does it frighten you?

TOD: What . . . frighten? I'm not frightened.

RUTH: It's not a threat.

TOD: I can only see the worst sort of pain, if you stay with her, Ruth. She's not responsible. It's not her fault, and very likely, she does love you. Just the same, I have to say, the bitch will wipe you out.

JOANNE: You'll only beat her to a bloody pulp?

TOD: I'll call you.

RUTH: Don't call me.

TOD: If you change your mind . . .

RUTH: I won't.

TOD: You know where to find me.

Silence.

TOD *opens the front door and walks out of the apartment.*

JOANNE: I love you, Ruth. But if you're going to bring your friends around, I hope you'll try and be a little more selective in the future. *(Slips the chain lock into place)* What are we going to do? Jump into bed, like Toddy said we would? I'd rather have dinner. I'm famished. What about you? Hey!

RUTH: I'm not hungry.

JOANNE: Don't let him get to you.

RUTH: It wasn't the same. He wasn't like . . .

JOANNE: The same as what?

RUTH: Wally. And Mike.

JOANNE: Oh, yes. No, it wasn't.

RUTH: It was more like . . . it made me think . . .

JOANNE: Don't think about it, Ruthie.

RUTH: *(Anger)* I think about it all the time. Sometimes, I think, the only real thing . . .

JOANNE: That's not true!

RUTH: One time, when Tod caught hold of me, I thought . . . I saw! Him. I was lying in the garbage, on my back, and he was sitting up on me. I could smell . . .

JOANNE: How do you keep all that pain inside you? Baby, you must have scarey dreams!

RUTH: I don't have dreams. I don't remember them.

JOANNE: How can you sleep on your own?

Silence.

RUTH: I wish I could stay here.

JOANNE: There's no hurry. What's the rush? It's early yet. You want to check the baby-sitter?

RUTH: I would have left the children on their own tonight! I must have tried a dozen people, agencies, you know? I couldn't get anyone to baby-sit. And I thought, I'm going out!

JOANNE: *(Laughing)* That's telling them!

RUTH: It's my life, too.

JOANNE: Way to go!

RUTH: It isn't true. I wouldn't leave the children on their own.

JOANNE: I know that.

RUTH: Anyway, it's not my life. At best, it's ours. Theirs and mine. No, I don't mean that. I'm not saying any of this right. I don't want to hurt your feelings.

JOANNE: What . . . hurt my feelings? How?

RUTH: I tell people things they want to hear. The way I think they want to hear them. In the end, I make more pain, because I go on and do exactly what I always meant to do, in just the way . . .

JOANNE: What are you trying to tell me?

RUTH: You feel threatened by the children.

JOANNE: They close me out, and leave me on my own.

RUTH: I don't think that's true.

JOANNE: When you're concentrating on the kids, you won't let yourself think about anything else. Anyone else!

RUTH: I try to make it seem they're not important, when I talk to you about them.

JOANNE: I can only say, you don't succeed.

RUTH: They are important.

JOANNE: Right.

RUTH: The most important!

JOANNE: Have I asked you to leave your kids? I can live with them. Figuratively speaking!

RUTH: And Steve. However much I make-believe, for your benefit, he was a part of my life for ten years. The best part! And he's still there, inside me.

JOANNE: You're not going back to him?

RUTH: No. I won't do that.

JOANNE: Thank God! For a moment there, you really had me worried.

Silence.

RUTH: I can't stay here.

JOANNE: Don't go yet. You haven't had anything to eat.

RUTH: I won't see you again.

JOANNE: Oh, yes.

RUTH: Not for some time.

JOANNE: That's what I thought you meant.

RUTH: It never has been real.

JOANNE: Depends on your point-of-view! It's real enough for me. You've been spending too much time with Toddy. Don't you know? It can't seem real to him.

RUTH: I lean on you, the way I used to lean on Steve. I let you take responsiblity for me.

JOANNE: You shouldn't listen to him.

RUTH: I want to share . . .

JOANNE: He's doing everything he can to take you away from me.

RUTH: If I can, now, stand on my own.

JOANNE: He wants you for himself.

RUTH: I can't substitute Joanne for Steve, and never let myself take on responsibility.

JOANNE: I should have kicked the ass-hole in the balls at lunch, and told him, "Keep your sticky hands off. She's mine!"

RUTH: I don't belong to you!

Silence.

RUTH: If I belong to anyone . . .

JOANNE: Those kids of yours!

RUTH: No, Joanne! To me!

Silence

RUTH: Of course, I don't. I belong to everyone, who's ever spoken to me, used me, taken hold me and put themselves into me, their words, their scum! The memory of all the captive minutes in my life! Time spent, listening, without learning, possessed, without being given anything, and left, afterwards, without gratitude, and no token of a pleasure, given, and received, in love. There's no love in me, Joanne.

JOANNE: That isn't true.

RUTH: It's not a contest. There's no choice. You and Tod! I'm not going to live with him.

JOANNE: He asked you to marry him.

RUTH: He didn't ask! He made love to me. Once ! And quickly! In his apartment, after lunch.

JOANNE: What was that number you did on me, before Tod got here?

RUTH: I was keeping something from you.

JOANNE: Going to bed with him?

RUTH: Yes. And I felt guilty.

JOANNE: That's my fault.

RUTH: Resentful!

JOANNE: I'm hip.

RUTH: It was so familiar. I thought, what is that!

JOANNE: You don't belong to me. You're right.

RUTH: She's not Steve. I don't have to keep things from Joanne. She'll understand.

JOANNE: What sort of things?

RUTH: I talked to Steve about us.

JOANNE: No! You didn't!

RUTH: He asked me why I was seeing so much of you.

JOANNE: What did you tell him?

RUTH: I said, I was in love with you.

JOANNE: I can't believe you'd do that!

RUTH: I don't think he was too happy. If I turn Lesbian, he'll never get me off his hands.

JOANNE: You go around, telling people?

RUTH: I don't keep it secret.

JOANNE: You said, Tod, and no one else.

RUTH: I was lying.

JOANNE: You do that a lot.

RUTH: I used to. Living with Steve, the only way I could protect myself. I don't have to now. I won't start again.

JOANNE: I make you tell lies? Is that what you're saying?

RUTH: Why don't you talk about me to your friends?

JOANNE: I talk about you.

RUTH: You don't tell them we've been lovers.

JOANNE: I only have that sort of conversation, Ruth, when I'm with you.

RUTH: You're ashamed.

JOANNE: I'm not ashamed!

RUTH: Why won't you let me meet them?

JOANNE: I have this feeling, if a lot of people get to know, they'll come and take you away from me. I guess that ass-hole Toddy knows more about me than I give him credit for knowing. I don't think all that much of myself, and there's a part of me wonders why you want to stay. Strike that! You don't. I'm sorry. You want to get out of here? Why don't you? Fuck off out! Doesn't that make it easy for you?

RUTH: You want me to go.

JOANNE: Oh, Christ!

RUTH: I'm not anything so special in your life.

JOANNE: You're not perfect. I'll do just as well without you, your dumb kids, ex-husband, fucked-up philosophy of life as a pain in the ass, which you put up with for no reason more than feeling bad makes you feel better! Shit! Can you imagine the life you might have, Ruth, if you ever let yourself feel good?

RUTH: Why try and keep me here? If I'm such a hopeless case, why can't you let me go?

JOANNE: I don't want you to leave me. I'll beg you to stay! If that's the game we're playing? I'm not proud. I don't want to lose you.

RUTH: You'll find someone else.

JOANNE: Sure! Why not? Anyone can be replaced. I don't want to replace you!

Silence.

RUTH: How can I get home? I don't want to walk.

JOANNE: You are going home?

RUTH: Yes.

JOANNE: Of course, you can't walk. Call a cab. There's a number. *(Picks up an address book and searches quickly for a number)* Are you sure you want to be on your own?

RUTH: I'm not on my own. I'm never, for one minute, on my own.

JOANNE: It's overrated. Here. *(Gives* RUTH *the address book)* I've had some experience, and I have to say, if Tod asked me to marry him, and the alternative was . . .

RUTH: You'd still be on your own. *(Picks up the receiver and dials a number)*

JOANNE: I can't disagree with that. I might get a dog.

RUTH: Will you send a taxi? . . . Two-twenty-two, West Fifty-third. Apartment 10A . . . The name's on the mail box. Carpenter. Tell him to ring and I'll come down . . . Yes, please. Right away. *(Puts down the receiver)*

JOANNE: You won't change your mind?

RUTH: Did I bring anything with me?

JOANNE: Not tonight.

RUTH: Have I left anything?

JOANNE: Not a lot. You want to look around?

RUTH: I guess so. If I leave things behind, you'll get to think I may come back.

JOANNE: That's a kid's game!

RUTH: I don't want there to be any misunderstanding.

JOANNE: No way!

RUTH *walks into the bedroom.*

JOANNE *turns, aimlessly, and looks for a pack of cigarettes. She picks up her purse and opens it. She starts to cry. The stronger lines of her face begin to weaken, and the child shows through.*

RUTH *walks into the living room.*

RUTH: There's too much for me to take. I'll have to come back. Is that all right?

JOANNE: Sure. Why not?

RUTH: Some time . . . when you're at the office . . .

JOANNE: Sounds good.

JOANNE *kneels down and gathers all the papers and photographs, collecting them together, and putting them into a file.*

RUTH: I'll wait downstairs.

JOANNE: No, you won't!

JOANNE *overreacts to* RUTH's *suggestion, and the emotion seems more like anger than concern for the other woman's welfare.*

JOANNE: You'll wait here. Right here! And when he gets here, then . . .

JOANNE *cannot complete her ultimatum, and she makes an indecisive, abrupt gesture, pointing at* RUTH, *awkwardly.*

RUTH: I don't want to make it any worse.

JOANNE: Oh, shit!

RUTH: You don't want me hanging around.

JOANNE: Will you stop telling me! That has to be your most annoying habit!

RUTH: I can't stand here . . .

JOANNE: Don't tell me what I want.

RUTH: . . . watching . . .

JOANNE: What I don't want! And if I want you to get out, believe me, Ace! I'll let you know.

RUTH: Don't shout at me!

JOANNE: I can see where, if I was a fella, I might want to punch you out. What is that? Something you program into your relationships? I have to tell you, Ruth, the longer I know you, the more I understand how people get to beating up on you.

RUTH: The longer I know you, Joanne, the easier it is to see why you're left on your own.

JOANNE: My sympathies are with the fellas.

RUTH: You don't want people close.

JOANNE: There you go!

RUTH: The moment somebody touches you . . .

JOANNE: If you can leave me . . .

RUTH: . . . you push them back.

JOANNE: Walk out of here . . .

RUTH: Make jokes.

JOANNE: . . . and I don't exist!

RUTH: Talk dirty!

JOANNE: You don't have to love . . .

RUTH: Who can love you?

JOANNE: . . . if you don't see me . . .

RUTH: I don't even like you.

JOANNE: Christ!

JOANNE reacts to RUTH's brutal declaration, as if it was a blow, delivered to the most vulnerable part of her body, and she slumps forward.

Instinctively, RUTH takes hold of JOANNE and comforts her.

JOANNE: You didn't really say that?

RUTH: Something else you taught me. Now, when I get angry . . .

JOANNE: It's not true?

RUTH: . . . I let it all hang out.

JOANNE: Is it true?

Silence.

RUTH: Not altogether.

JOANNE: Some?

RUTH: Yes.

JOANNE: For old times' sake, you want to make an exception in my case, and tell a few lies? If the truth has got to be so brutal, I'm not sure how well I can cope with it.

RUTH: What truth: I'm just another crazy lady. You triggered a response and the accumulated bitterness of thirty, blah,blah, years came pouring out. It could be you I don't like. Just as well, Steve. Wally, Mike, Toddy, or the kids. Maria! My life is filled with people who make me angry, and I'm only now beginning to work out why that is. It's got less to do with you, than with the young man in the alley, and my need of him, my needing to be hurt, degraded and humiliated, because that ass-hole, Steve, could make me feel like a dumb cunt, useless and unattractive, and anyway, why did I marry Steve? I didn't have much ambition, if I settled for him, and I did have ambition! I wanted beauty, I hoped for as much truth, and most of all, justice.

JOANNE: The whole cartoon strip! Wouldn't you know? As for me! You've heard about those kids who used to surf around the world, looking for the perfect wave? I'm thirty, blah, blah, blah! And I'm still hanging in there, looking for the perfect fuck! I'm about ready to give up. What do you think?

RUTH: You're fighting some kind of war.

JOANNE: I'm not winning.

RUTH: It's not my war.

The house telephone rings.

RUTH: And if it is, I'm not ready for it. *(Picks up the receiver of the house telephone)* Yes? . . . I'll be right down.

JOANNE: Send him away.

RUTH *hangs up the receiver.*

RUTH: I don't want to stay here.

JOANNE There's no answer to that.

RUTH: There's too much of you I don't want to share. You feed my anger.

JOANNE: You should be angry. Don't we have good reason?

RUTH: It's my choice, and I can't accept the loss of feeling, my capacity for gentleness, vulnerability. I can't be tougher than they are, just to let them know I can be tough.

JOANNE: Show them you're vulnerable, they'll beat the shit out of you.

The house telephone buzzes.

JOANNE: Suppose old faithful Toddy's waiting on the doorstep?

RUTH: I'll kick him in the balls!

JOANNE *laughs and raises one hand in a salute.*

RUTH *unhooks the chain lock and opens the door. She steps out of the apartment and closes the door.*

JOANNE *looks for a pack of cigarettes without any great sense of purpose.*

JOANNE: Oh, shit! *(Perches on the arm of the sofa)* Whatever!

[END OF ACT THREE]

Appendix

ACT THREE

In the first draft of the play, RUTH's monologue, on page 105, was presented in a far more complex form. It was intended to dramatize RUTH's life, from childhood to young womanhood, on to her marriage, and ending at her encounter with the man in the alley. It also included references to the day-to-day ugliness which surrounds us in urban life, where we are so often the victims of another's thoughtless obscenity, and lack of concern for anyone else's sensibilities.

The monologue was compressed for the production in New York, which was essentially naturalistic, and could not support the state of suspended time which would allow for the full development of RUTH's anguish. In a more stylized production, where the stress is not so firmly placed on such a realistic setting, it might be possible to use the longer version, and so, I offer it here. If a director should favor this form of the monologue, I hope he will discuss with me the opportunities it presents to display RUTH more fully, and the way it should be incorporated into the play as a whole, before making his final decision.

J.H.

RUTH *pulls away from* JOANNE.

RUTH: Animals! Like animals! Not people. Making pain! Listen! Why must people? Can't you hear yourselves? Loving, why can't you be more, and not anger, all the time, hating! I hate the goddamn house. I always have! Ruthie . . .

The single word 'hate' plunges RUTH *into the memory, and down into the confrontation between* STEVE *and herself.*

RUTH's *voice reflects the emotional state of each speaker. She does not imitate their vocal qualities, or their individual mannerisms.* RUTH *becomes the speaker, and the speaker is always recognizably* RUTH.

RUTH: . . . I hate the people! All the goddamn, interfering neighbors. Shit! I spend my life around a bunch of people I despise. You want to know the truth? You got us out here. It was your idea. You bought the fucking house. I paid for it! You found it. You bought it. Christ! What am I doing? Living like this! You know how old I am? Jesus Christ! Don't shout at me. You can talk to me like a reasonable human being. You don't have to shout. I shout at you, because you don't hear me, Ruthie, if I treat you like a reasonable human being! You've got so much junk rattling around that empty head of yours. Shit! Right now, you think I might wake up the kids, with all this shouting, and you're only listening out for them. You don't hear a word I'm saying. You don't hear a fucking word! You're so dumb! Don't speak to your sister like that. He broke it on purpose. No, I didn't. Yes, you did. Didn't. Did! He was playing with my horses, and he broke my favorite. My palomino! He broke it on purpose. I did not!

The transition between one moment in time and another occurs without any perceptible pause.

If you can't play together, without quarrelling! I hate you. It's not my fault. I hope you go to hell! I didn't touch the goddamn horse! I hope you die and go to hell! You blame me for everything. I hope you die. It isn't fair. I hate you . . .

The words muddle together, in a jumble of incomprehensible anger and hostility, until, finally, in despair, RUTH *cries out.*

Silence.

RUTH: You can't stay up there all day, Ruthie. Don't be silly. Mama hit me. She was angry, darling. She didn't mean to hurt you. She hit me, and we don't hit people in this house. Come on down and we can talk to Mommy. Ruthie, won't you? Just for me. Please. I'm afraid you might fall. You come and get me, Daddy. Well, I don't know. It looks awful high for an old guy to climb up there. I'll come down. *(Singing)* "Deep river, my home is over Jordan. Deep river, Lord, I want to cross over into camp ground." Why did you send Daddy away? What did he do? Will you let him come back soon? Is he cross with us, Mommy? Is it something . . . did I do . . . something? Did I make him angry? Is that why Daddy went away? I don't know what I did. Do you know, Mommy? *(Singing)* "Coming for to carry me home."

Silence.

JOANNE: Ruthie.

RUTH: If you paid attention and didn't sit around all day, with your mouth open and your eyes shut, dreaming about boys! I can't think why we try to educate girls like you. The first thing, when you leave college, you'll get pregnant, if not before! You'll get married, and you'll never open another book the rest of your life. I pity the man you marry. What sort of wife will you make? What sort of mother? I pity your children. *(Singing)* "Steal away, steal away . . . "

RUTH *gasps audibly, and her eyes open wide.*

RUTH: No. Not here. Why not, Ruthie? I don't want to. Nobody can see us. I don't want to . . . do it. What sort of game are you playing with me? You've been letting me think all evening! I've changed my mind. You're going to do it, baby. Now, you're going to do it! It's different for a boy, Ruth. You must always remember. I'm going to have your ass! Some boys are so big, they can't fit inside a normal girl. I don't believe that! Elizabeth-Jane told me. Oh, well! She saw her brother in the bathroom, and he was . . . you know? What do you mean, Mama? How is it different? She saw him? Yes, she did. And was it . . . really big? Enormous! Oh, I don't believe anything Elizabeth-Jane says. Get off your ass, Ruthie! It's a two-way street, getting laid! You want to get some of the action? And did he . . . you know? Yes! I wish I had a brother. Oh, shit! I'm going to come! Cindy let her boyfriend go all the way last weekend, at the lake. Cindy Parker! She told me all about it. Is she pregnant? You should never encourage a boy past a certain point. You should never let him get too excited. You're not going to tell me you're a virgin, Ruthie? Shit!

RUTH *starts to laugh.*

RUTH: Kisses, clumsy fingers, pushing in between my legs, pushing into me, and his thing. He couldn't wait for me. He pushed in, and he came, and I didn't feel anything. Some momentary pain, I can remember, and the humiliation, like what we did was, somehow, shameful, and we wouldn't ever talk about it, and we never did. He must have told his friends. They never treated me in quite the same way afterwards. He never talked to me. Never really talked. I knew what he looked like, with his jeans pushed down around his ankles. I knew what happened to his thing. I watched it shrink back into itself. I watched him scramble into the front seat and try to hide his pathetic nakedness. I felt sorrow for him. I could feel his flesh inside my flesh. It was my first time, and I won't forget one minute of the ugly degradation, lying on my back, with my skirt bundled up around my waist, my panties torn and dragged to one side and my legs, stuck up in the air, the sweating smell, the suffocating heat, inside that car, on that back seat, and if I look down far enough into my memory, I can find the marks the leather buttons made on my buttocks. Eighteen, I guess, going on nineteen. *(Singing)* "Deep river . . ." I don't know how you could have done it, Ruth. I always thought you had more self-respect. I can't pretend we're not shocked. Your mother and I. Some of your college friends, I guess, they must think we're pretty old-fashioned. *(Singing)* " . . . want to cross over into camp ground . . ." One good thing, he didn't get you pregnant. Nobody has to know? Don't you be smart with me, young woman! I guess you want people to know? Do you? *(Singing)* "Deep river, Lord . . ."

RUTH *starts to cry.*

RUTH: I don't think we can let you go back to college, Ruth, if we can't trust you to behave like a decent young woman. If we have to worry every minute, what you might be doing. *(Singing)* "Michael, row the boat ashore . . ." Face it, Ruth. You're not the most exciting fuck I ever had. I don't want to hurt your feelings. Just the same, you have to know, if I went looking for someone else, it wasn't my fault, altogether. You won't deny that? *(Singing)* "Sister, help to trim the sails, Halelujah!" We had some good times in bed? Oh, sure. More or less in spite of you, I always had the feeling. I couldn't really know. You wouldn't talk about it. Any time I did, like I was pissing in church! *(Singing)* "Jordan's river is deep and wide . . ." It's different now. For old times' sake, getting into bed together, once in a while. You know what? I think you're trying harder. That's weird! All those years we were married. Honey, believe me! You only get back what you're ready to put out. Nothing for nothing! You know what I'm saying? I don't know why I waste my time! You can't play worth a shit! If you'd made some sort of effort. Learn the fundamentals! *(Singing)* "Meet my brother on the other side. Hallelujah!" You don't lead from a king and then leave yourself naked. Christ! Of course, he's going to finesse your ace. Once he knows where it is, you don't have a hope in hell. You're so fucking stupid! The kids understand more about the game than you do. At least, they play like they want to win. The objective is to beat them. You're my partner. You're not supposed to make it easier for them to kick the shit out of us! What were you thinking about all evening? Was Tom groping you under the table? Did he have his hand up your skirt? Is that what was on your mind? He's welcome! Shit! If he only knew! He's better off with Jenny, and Christ knows! She's the second Ice Age. You can't get into her with a lever! *(Singing)* "Michael, row the boat ashore . . . " Tom says, fucking her is like screwing a water hole in the Painted Desert. 'Course, he doesn't worry. He was telling me about this girl he's got. Sounds like a regular dumb cunt! Still, you've got to say, she gives him value. He didn't tell me what he pays her. He told me what they do, and any way you slice it, he's getting value! You want me to tell you, Ruthie? You want to fool around? You want to get off? You want to fuck? Hey, lady! Pretty nice tits! You got time for a quickie? Why don't we go to your place? I'll show you a good time. What's your hurry? Where are you going? Hey! You want to get hold of that? You want to let me grab your ass!

RUTH *allows* JOANNE *to approach her.*

RUTH: She's no better than a whore. She puts out for anyone. All she thinks about is getting laid. You take it out and put it in her hand. She does the rest. I wouldn't marry any girl, if I knew she put out for other guys. I guess, you must be queer for women. That's the reason, right? I got to say, it's a fucking waste! With a body on you like that. Takes a man to appreciate! I bet you never had a real man. You want to try me? Baby, I'll set you straight. You know it! Open your mouth up, cunt. You know what to do. Get on with it, and easy with the teeth.

JOANNE *takes hold of* RUTH.

JOANNE *recognizes the reference to the man who attacked* RUTH *in the alley, and she tries to prevent the memory from taking hold of* RUTH's *agonized imagination.*

RUTH: *(Singing)* "Deep river, my home . . . " When Daddy fucks you, baby, you know you've been fucked. *(Singing)* " . . . home is over Jordan . . . " I don't know how you could have done it, Ruth. I always thought you had more self-respect. You get your ass over here! Put your money where you mouth is!

RUTH *starts to laugh. The sound is ugly and painful to hear.*

RUTH: Get over! Roll over! On your belly! He won't be able to resist. That doesn't hurt. Lie still. Relax. You know it doesn't really hurt. The sensible girl is always prepared for the unexpected. That's good. Oh, yes. Oh, baby! *(Singing)* " . . . cross over into camp ground . . . " I love you. It's not a question of respect. I really love you. There's nothing wrong, when two people love each other. *(Singing)* " . . . cross over into . . . " Do you love me? Shit, baby! I love you. You know that. I love your ass. You've got the greatest ass. I think about your ass all day. I can't wait! Can you be sure? Will he still respect you afterwards? In the circumstance, the wisest course! At least, he didn't get you pregnant. Christ, Ruth! You were going to take precautions. I don't want another kid. I can't afford the one we've got. Anyway, bringing kids up in the city! What sort of a life is that for them? We'll have to move. We can't have another kid in this apartment. Shit! You were going to make sure. You know I hate to wear a rubber! *(Singing)* "My home is over Jordan . . . " Why didn't Daddy come and see us? He promised. This weekend, he said. He was going to take me to a movie, and out to dinner. Why didn't you let him come and see me? I don't want to live with you. I want to go and live with my Daddy.

RUTH *begins to shake.*

RUTH: I don't love you any more.

RUTH *murmurs the melody of "Deep River" softly to herself.*

RUTH: Hmm, mm, mm, mm, mm . . . mm, mm, mm, mm, mm, mm, mm . . . mm, mm, mm, mm, mm . . . Lord . . .

Silence.

Tod: She can't stay here.

Joanne: Get out of here, Tod.

Their mutual concern for Ruth *moderates the violence of their antagonism for a time.*

By TISH DACE

LOSING TIME. AT THE MANHATTAN THEATRE CLUB, 321 E. 73RD ST.. 472-0600.

John Hopkins' corrosive study of sexual degradation known as *Losing Time* has something to offend both men and women, both the political **right and the left. When Shir**ley Knight as Ruth wails that she *wanted* the stranger in the alley to force his "thing" into her mouth, she could well start a stampede to the exit, as the squeamish and the feminist outraged by suggestions that women want to be raped vie to see who can be the first out the door.

This Strindbergian treatment of women's rites of passage from masochism to self-respect, from dependence to independence is daring, dangerous, and easy to put down. Yet it is also an important play which, despite inevitably hostile reviews, will find an appreciative audience. Painful it is. Harrowing it is. Ugly it is. And, yes, shocking it is, even to people of unrefined sensitivities. But which of us doesn't go to the theatre hoping maybe this time the play will be powerful? Well, this time it is.

Some spectators' insecurities will force them to erect barriers against the pain—just as they did at John Guare's devastating *Bosoms and Neglect* last spring—but, for those in touch with their feelings, *Losing Time* is not just a fine play. It is also a therapeutic expression of the mutual hostility many men and women are beginning to recognize, articulate—and exorcise.

Losing Time's loser becomes, not a winner, but at least a woman who no longer wears a figurative sign reading "knock me down." Indeed this born loser (anatomy is destiny?) ends the play not only making her own decisions but exercising some control over others' options as well. If nobody's a winner in lust, some, Hopkins could be suggesting, may at least learn to achieve autonomy.

Hopkins takes his time turning a self-destructive hysteric into a reasonable facsimile of a human being, and he makes the process of transformation from doormat to person unsettling and sometimes unpleasant. Under the tutelage of Jane Alexander's wise-cracking lover Joanne, Ruth moves from suffering psychic blows to inflicting them, and we are offered no guidance by Hopkins to the interpretation of this second act sexual warfare until the scene's end. Meantime, the women put their dates through all sorts of sexual humiliation: exploiting their bodies while giving neither affection nor respect; groping them; denigrating their potency; and making gross sexual advances which communicate no interest in any aspect of their company save their ability in bed. One infers that Ruth and Joanne have adopted the exploitative manners to which they've been subjected by men in the past, but Hopkins never lets them say so in words. Only their exultant screams after the men's departure express, obliquely, the rationale behind their brutal ball-breaking.

Although this isn't a pretty picture of women, it's no more anti-woman than anti-male.

More importantly, it's not anti-human, though some intelligent viewers may perceive it that way. Outraged devotees of marriage may parade pieties about its sanctity or deplore Hopkins' obscenities and violence all they like. They can't change the fact that battering— physical and psychological— occurs in a shocking number of relations betwen ostensibly respectable men and women. *Losing Time* makes us confront contemporary sexual antagonisms. And it hints that, if men and women recover their self-esteem, they might later come together in harmony again. Yet Hopkins makes no case; he puts questions, but supplies no pat answers.

It took two brave couples to bring such a largely pessimistic view of coupling to the stage: the author and his wife Shirley Knight playing one leading role, and director Edwin Sherin along with his wife Jane Alexander in the other.

These key roles are unbelievably demanding. Knight is asked to tumble in the door spotted with mud and blood and announce, without one second to build to it, that she's been raped. She brings it off— and still leaves room for Ruth to reach a contained rage farther into the first act, where she gives us a stunning and completely natural piece of acting. Later Ruth's cool determination to live as she decrees nicely sets off the tears of her hitherto self-assured lover. As that bisexual lover, Jane Alexander assures that her cynical wit and strong will aren't perceived as negative— or even masculine—characteristics. And she makes credible a crumbling poise, a not entirely unexpected vulnerability, for just as a masochist can cease to crave pain, a liberated woman can cease to block it. Although Alexander's role at first may be the hardest to sympathize with, before she's done with us it becomes the most accessible. And Tom Mardirosian, Bernie McInerney and Tony Roberts play various male chauvinist types with a conviction which suggests they recognize the occasional female chauvinism of their adversaries.

OOKING-GLASS

by Michael Sutton and Cynthia Mandelberg

This provocative chronicle, interspersed with fantasy sequences from ALICE IN WONDERLAND, traces the career of Charles Dodgson (better known as Lewis Carroll) from his first work on the immortal classic, to his downfall when accused of immortality.

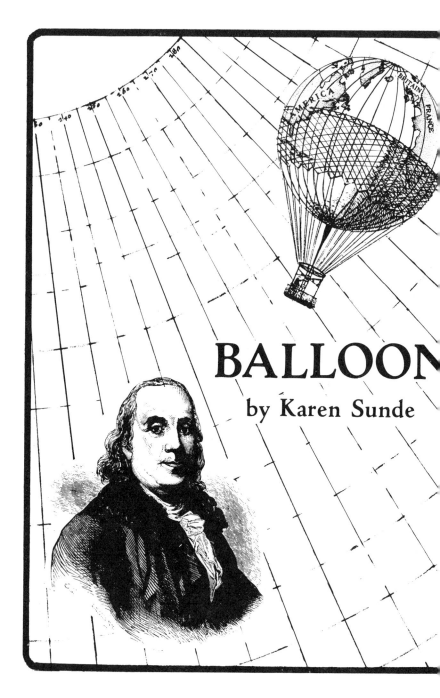

BALLOON

by Karen Sunde

Benjamin Franklin, American Ambassador to Paris during the 18th Century, plays host to his French contemporaries during a festive parlor visit, while the fates of nations hang in the balance.

SOME RAIN

by James Edward Luczak

Set in rural Alabama in 1968, the play is the bittersweet tale of a middle-aged waitress whose ability to love and be loved is re-kindled by her chance encounter with a young drifter. First presented in 1982 at the Eugene O'Neill Playwright's Conference and Off-Broadway on Theatre Row.

ESCOFFIER
KING OF CHEFS
by
Owen S. Rackleff

In this one-man show set in a Monte Carlo villa at the end of the last century, the grand master of the kitchen, Escoffier, ponders a glorious return from retirement. In doing so, he relates ancedotes about the famous and shares his mouth-watering recipes with the audience.

DEATH in the POT

by Manuel Van Loggem

An English-style thriller with a fascinating plot that takes intricate twists and turns, as a husband and wife try to kill each other off, aided by a mysterious Merchant of Death. Mr. Van Loggem's works have been widely produced throughout Europe.

BATTERY

BY DANIEL THERRIAULT

Electricity is the central metaphor and an expressive image
for this unusual love story set in an electrical workshop.

PLAYS FROM
BROADWAY PLAY PUBLISHING, IN

(See inside back cover)

BALLOON
by Karen Sunde

BATTERY
by Daniel Therriault

DEATH IN THE POT
by Manuel Van Loggem

ESCOFFIER: KING OF CHEFS
by Owen S. Rackleff

LOOKING GLASS
by Cynthia Mandelberg and Michael Sutton

LOSING TIME
by John Hopkins

SOME RAIN
by James Edward Luczak

ISBN: 0-88145-0